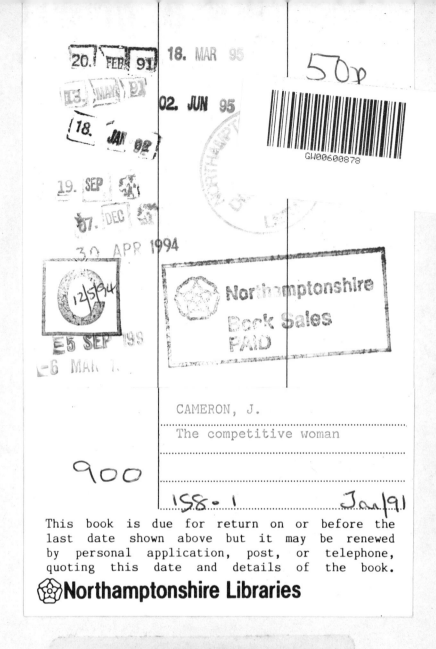

Kathy Burkee

THE COMPETITIVE WOMAN

A Survival Guide for the Woman
Who Aims to be Boss

Janet Cameron

MERCURY

First published in 1988
by Mercury Books

Published in paperback 1990
by Mercury Books
Gold Arrow Publications Ltd
862 Garratt Lane, London SW17 0NB

Set in Palatino by Phoenix Photosetting,
Printed and bound in Great Britain by
Butler & Tanner Ltd, Frome and London

ISBN 1 85252 086 8

For their empathy, their practical
help and their encouragement, I
would like to acknowledge and
thank, in alphabetical order,

Marita Boulton
Gloria Ferris
Rennie Fritchie
Marilyn Hunter
Maggie of Warlingham
Derrick Mardle
My Mother
Maureen Sampson
Deryn Stewart
Anne Watts

Also my sons, Marc and Gareth,
for being proud of the business
and for making tea when I was
busy.

CONTENTS

INTRODUCTION

Venue – my client's boardroom. My role – consultant. Purpose of meeting – to help co-ordinate the new promotional brochure for his company. Result – I had finally managed to interpret my client's requirements and translate them into practicalities. As I rose, so did he, a distinguished middle-aged man in a sober, well cut suit.

'Why *do* you run your own business?' he asked in genuine wonderment.

'Because it's necessary for me to work and I prefer to work for myself than for someone else,' I replied, as I replaced the copy and transparencies in my portfolio.

He followed me to the lift.

'Well, I suppose it's better than kicking your heels around the house all day,' he muttered.

'I do so agree with you,' I conceded sweetly. 'It simply wouldn't make economic good sense. The only trouble is, home helps are *so* hard to find. Do you know anyone who might be interested? A nice young man would do, I'm not sexist.'

If he looked a little subdued as we shook hands, I could not help but notice a sudden twinkle in his eye as I stepped into the lift.

It helps a lot if you can maintain your sense of humour when confronted with situations like this – if you can turn the tables with a joke. Anger would have alienated him, possibly lost me a client and a source of income. This is not meant in any way to deny the value of forcefulness when circumstances call for it. (Better to be thought a little 'pushy' than get a reputation as a 'pushover'.) Personally I like to 'play it by ear' and I have found that gentle self-assertiveness can be tremendously effective.

Many women dislike the idea of getting on in business by aping male characteristics. They wish to be successful business people with their own female persona intact.

In this book I shall tell you about the business techniques that have worked for me and for other successful women, in the hope that you may find them useful, and that you may take from them and adapt them to suit your own style and personality.

While my experience is mainly in office supplies (still a male preserve), both in ready-made products and in manufacturing, I maintain that 95 per cent of these principles can easily be applied to other fields. Therefore this book is aimed at the woman who wishes either to elevate her status as an employee with an established company or organisation, or who intends to venture into business under her own steam.

This is not a book for superwomen, but for ordinary women like me who would like to achieve control over their own lives and destiny. The only qualification I have for writing this book is my own hard won experience.

My education at an ordinary state comprehensive was completed at 16 years. I started my business with nothing but a poky, mortgaged flat in a far from salubrious part of South London, with little money, an ancient but reliable Volkswagen Beetle and lacking even the luxury of a telephone. Twelve years later I have a business turning over in excess of £100,000 a year and nobody telling me what to do.

'Why do you run your own business?'

Well, it *is* better than kicking your heels around the house all day, even if you can afford to indulge yourself so freely. But more than that, I started my own business because I wanted to, because I wanted control over my own life and rewards for my efforts.

How?

There is no great mystery. In a nutshell you need a fairly thick skin, utter determination, unflagging optimism and the ability to take the early, regular defeats with resignation.

Yes, resignation. Not a word usually bandied about in books about business. But it is pertinent to remember that losing the occasional battle does not prevent you from winning the war.

So muster your troops (determination, optimism and resignation) and read on . . .

1

SNAKES AND LADDERS

Men often ask me if it is easier in business being a woman. My reply is that I could not possibly know, having never experienced being in business as a man.

A lot depends on whether they mean 'Is it easier in business because one is a woman?' or 'Is it easier *getting on* in business as a woman?' Working from my own observations, I would say the answer is unavoidably 'no' to the latter question. It is definitely not easier for a woman if she wishes to progress and take an active, competing role.

I asked one successful young female manager.

'I started off as a secretary with my company, but when I saw all the reps around me, meeting people, getting *involved*, I knew that was all I wanted to do.

'When a new selling vacancy arose, I applied for it. My boss interviewed me as if I was an outsider, which was fair enough. What *was* unreasonable was that my interview was tougher because I was a woman. He behaved to me as if he was a very awkward customer, trying to shock me to see how I would handle sexual harassment.

'Another point I resented was that he wanted to know all about my "ties". My company prefers it if their male executives are married, but the females must be single.

'So I became their first woman rep and they have since taken on another. Single, of course.'

So how did she cope out in the field?

[12]

'There are pitfalls. It is sometimes difficult for a woman to be taken seriously, especially by an older, professional man. I try to get over this by impressing them with my product knowledge and experience. I tell them that I have been with my company for 10 years which seems to give them some feeling of stability.'

I compared her experiences with my own first appointment as a sales representative some years ago, where the training was orientated to provoke sexual harassment rather than repel it.

'Leave the top button of your blouse undone, keep crossing and uncrossing your legs to help distract your client.' Those were the words that propelled me into taking the plunge and starting my own business. Although women have undoubtedly made progress, it is obvious that there is still a long way to go.

Despite my reaction to the above sexist advice, I am not suggesting that a woman should deny her femininity and operate like a hard-line feminist; indeed such a 'bulldozing' approach would be incompatible with the technique of a commercially aware businesswoman. Men are not demeaned by the use of a soft-sell approach, and some use this less assertive method of progression quite successfully.

A woman too can choose the option of charm and persuasion, providing she can be firm too. Then, if she does decide to get tough when the situation calls for it, she will have more impact than if she persistently throws her weight around all the time.

Industry and commerce are still predominantly male, white, middle-aged and middle-class. It is necessary to 'find oneself', to work out one's style and ways of adapting to a relatively new environment, which is still on occasion a hostile one. There are few precedents to fall back on and in some areas probably none.

The chances are you may not be fortunate enough to find a mentor of your own sex and few opportunities to observe successful patterns of behaviour in other executive women.

You can of course partly compensate for this by joining one of the women's support groups.

Therefore survival in business can be a difficult assault course, so recognise the snakes and the ladders on the way up. It can help a lot.

Here are some of the problems that different women have faced – and their reactions:

- 'I worked for a company once that suddenly expanded and they had to bring in a new job-grading system. My job was quite a good one at the time and highly placed on the original scale and that would mean under the new system I would become quite a powerful force within the set-up. My male associates were frantic. Stage One was a meeting, from which I was excluded. All the managers came down to London, from as far afield as Scotland and the Midlands, just to try and find a way to re-grade my job down. I was horrified when I found out, I just couldn't believe it.'

- 'I love my job and I'm pleased I've got on so well in my company. The only thing is, there is one manager who is always singling me out for comment. He doesn't do it to any of the men, only me. He keeps saying, "Isn't it time you packed up and got married?" I think that somehow he sees me as more of a threat because I am a woman and because I have achieved a lot. I try to reassure him and convince him I am not a threat.'

- 'I find that men try to shock me, not necessarily as a line of chat, but just to see how far they can go, to see if I can *take* it. I don't let it get under my skin. I brush it aside, make a joke or pretend I haven't noticed.'

In these three examples you will find the following tactics:

The conspiracy – that insidious, collective strategy calculated to deprive you of the power you have earned.

The heckling – a subtle form of mental Chinese torture, seemingly harmless but intended, in its sheer persistency, to undermine your authority.

The shock treatment – the sudden unexpected jabs designed to puncture your self-assurance.

Nevertheless one must take a balanced view and realise that there are a great many males who would be horrified at these methods. In addition there are sometimes positive advantages in being a woman, if only one is aware of them and willing to apply them:

- 'As a saleswoman, the main advantage is that when I call on a male client, I am always *seen*. It's probably curiosity. I am confident of my abilities and strength. I know I am a good organiser and that I can sell. *Knowing* that I can get in, I am halfway to getting an order. I also find in my team that the men are not always so deft at administration – they're easily bored with paperwork and often fail to follow things through.'

- 'Men will confide in a woman where they might hold back with other men. It is important to behave with them as an equal, not inferior, not better, but as an *equal*. Then it's easy to negotiate, to get them to talk to you. Sometimes you can find out useful information about what's going on in your company, which can give you an edge over the men.'

Making the Most of Your Natural Resources

Men may be devious, but, make no mistake, we women have the edge in this respect. Owing to our sex's long history of subjugation, cunning is inborn. It was one of the few weapons our female ancestors possessed and is part of our evolution, like *homo sapiens'* tail-less and upright stature. Why should all those years of oppression have been in vain?

Let your foxy shrewdness and ingenuity work for you in business. This inbuilt advantage, together with confidence and knowhow, will provide you with all that you need to progress and win.

It is not necessary to belittle or try to emasculate men without provocation. Most of my business dealings have been with men, and although I have had painful experiences, in retrospect I have also enjoyed a number of 'lucky breaks'. A man with a proper sense of self-respect and no ego problems does not need to oppose others on grounds of sex, race or creed, and it does make life simpler to give the benefit of the doubt until proved wrong.

So do whatever you must do, but keep a sense of proportion. If you meet opposition, in whatever guise, try to find a way to push it aside and make a space for yourself.

Your natural cunning is your best defence while preparing to progress and win.

2

RUSSIAN ROULETTE OR A GAME OF CHESS?

In business of course everyone has to take chances. Nothing is guaranteed. You have to weigh up all the pros and cons and then you have to make a decision. Otherwise you will just stand still. You won't fail, but you won't succeed either.

Don't play Russian Roulette. Whatever course you take, try to leave yourself an 'out' if it all goes wrong. Conduct yourself in business as you would in a game of chess, protecting your pieces to enable you to attack – and checkmate.

Allies

While it is essential to 'suss out' the opposition and to take this into your calculations, it is equally desirable to seek out like-minded souls – in other words, those who understand your potential and would like to assist you in your progress by acting as mentor, ally or adviser.

Do, however, for your own protection, consider their possible motives:

(a) *Loyalty to the Company*
   This is a sound reason for helping you. If the company prospers, the more power to the elbow of your ally –

until, that is, you are doing so well that you pose a
threat to your ally's position. Then watch out!

(b) *Mutual Progress*
Maybe your ally needs you as much as you need him/
her. You can relax, at least, until one of you ceases to
depend upon the other.

(c) *Mutual Liking and Respect*
If your status is on a par with that of your ally, be ready
for a change of heart if you are suddenly promoted over
his or her head. Unless your ally is a true friend, your
mutual rapport may become clouded with tension, even
hostility.

Boardroom Groupies

It is essential to understand something about how business
operates and what makes people tick. The attitudes of businessmen towards executive or self-made women merit consideration.

The term 'Boardroom Groupies' is intended to describe
hangers-on in the form of buffers and incompetents who
baffle, confuse and irritate with their misguided ideas about
how to get to the top and how to prevent you from joining them
there, but who are for the time being senior to you in status.

To get what you want you must learn the techniques of
dealing with difficult people. There will be times when this
will go against your natural inclinations and the ability to be
totally objective will be a useful tool in assisting you to keep
your cool, react in a rational manner and, most important,
progress. Never forget that *progressing* with a view of *winning* is
your objective.

But don't worry. When you are the boss, it will be a
different story.

[18]

The crawler

The crawler is a boardroom groupie of the first order, yet how can one not feel anything but a sneaking sympathy for this unfortunate character? He is terribly insecure in his job (in fact his boss knows he's a bit of a twit) and everything has to be right and exact for Mr Bigboots, his boss. Every 't' crossed and 'i' dotted.

If Mr Bigboots says around Monday will be OK, the crawler will insist, 'We want it done Monday, no later. Otherwise you can forget it. What do you mean, it's impossible? Ridiculous! I don't know what I'll say to Mr Bigboots.'

On the telephone you can almost hear sharp intakes of breath down the earpiece and you're not sure if it is line interference or Mr Bigboots breathing down the crawler's neck.

Handling. Accept that the crawler understands no other system. Such compulsive behaviour, based on feelings of inadequacy, is difficult if not impossible to change. Avoid his company as far as possible, reassure him as much as is reasonable, and, bearing in mind he is senior to you in status, suppress any urge to grumble about him to your colleagues.

Even the hapless crawler has his pride.

The egotist

He'll go on and on . . . endlessly: his three cars, his two boats, the fillings he had put in his teeth last week, the MP he spoke to last night, his American agency, his new business project in Timbuctoo. He is of course the leading man in his field. Why, from all over the world it is said 'this is the man who . . .' etc., etc.

He can't afford to be bothered by trivialities. After all, he makes over £3,000 per deal.

Handling. Try to look interested, nod your head every so often and think of England. Although he has a 'boardroom groupie' mentality, some of what he says may be true and he could be a groupie who's made it.

[19]

When he has finished, if he ever does, he is sure to have forgotten why you were there in the first place. Leave him in no doubt, and be as forceful as he is about the validity of giving you your rise/promotion/order.

The time waster

It isn't difficult to arrange an appointment to see the time waster. No one is ever turned away, and his superficially easy-going attitude is endorsed by a joke postcard on his door reading 'We Shoot Every Third Rep – the Second One has Just Left'.

The time waster thrives on trivia. He is smart, dapper and genuinely likes women (except in responsible business positions). He will enjoy his little chat with you, during which his life history and personal achievements will be aired for your entertainment and appreciation.

He may even make one or two vague promises, but whether he will ever honour them is a moot point. However, he will certainly never say 'no' outright, and is the guy who will most frequently observe how much easier it must be for you in business, since you are a woman.

Handling. With the right approach and lots of patience maybe he can be converted to your way of thinking, although it would be wise to research his true power quotient before embarking on such a project. Try not to let him waste too much of your time, which could be better spent cultivating more worthwhile business contacts.

The sycophant

'Well, helloooooo! What have we here? What's a pretty girl like you doing . . . ?' etc.

It is just a dreadful habit, I am sure. So many men feel they have to adopt a line of chat when conversing with a woman, be they secretary, business colleague or sometimes even their boss. They seem convinced that their repartee must be peppered with compliments and other signals of approval. This line of defence, for that is what it is, seems to be more common in older men. It is probably how they once chatted up their girl friends. Maybe they still do.

If you are operating in a male-dominated field, your contact may be particularly prone to revert to this comfortingly tried and trusted method of covering up what may be merely shyness or discomfort.

Handling. Try not to fidget. Thank him briefly and get on to another subject: his holidays and what he's doing for Christmas. If you know him well enough, a good ruse is to get him on to discussing his wife and kids.

Do take comfort from the fact that whatever the psychological reasons for his inadequacy, his boss must get just as sick of him as you do, and when he's calmed down, you can get down to business.

The whiner

Nothing is ever right for him. Like the egotist, he is an utter bore concerning, say, his tax problems, his idiot staff, his incompetent accountant, his nervous bank manager. Every two or three seconds his voice is pitched two octaves higher.

Handling. It may be said that the best line of defence is attack, but not in his case. Conjuring up a blacker cat will not deter him, but only serve to increase his ardour. Handle him as for the egotist, and think of England, and America . . . and the Balkans . . . and Japan . . .

3

SELLING AS A MEANS TO PROGRESSING AND WINNING

Several years ago, when I was a young mum in need of some cash and an outside interest, my friend Barbara and I got together and made oven gloves on her sewing machine. Bright ginghams and florals cut from discarded dresses and curtains were used for the outers, and the silk and nylon for the inners came from people's old knickers and nighties.

We presented them beautifully, mounted on glossy white card with a cellophane wrapper.

Friends and relatives sold them for us at their places of work, but one young lady in particular had enormous success. We couldn't get production moving fast enough. The floor was permanently covered in bits of foam, material, tapes and sellotape. The kids were left to their own devices as we frantically cut, ironed, sewed and packed.

The secret of her success?

She simply told her colleagues that the gloves were made by a dear little old lady who couldn't make ends meet on her pension.

Barbara and I were ashamed of this barefaced lie. But what wicked wit and imagination! If it could have been applied to business proper, she would have made a fortune.

There must be a wealth of untapped female talent in offices and factories.

Confidence

First of all, I think it is necessary to accept that lack of confidence is perfectly natural, especially when encountering some new or untried situation. If you make a *faux pas*, never quit. Struggle through to the end, making as light of it as possible, and keep cool. If you can laugh at yourself, openly and without guile, then that is even better.

Once I froze, immobilised by nerves, having started a pre-rehearsed little speech and having gone terrifyingly mentally blank in an office full of people I was desperate to impress. They laughed, but not unkindly, and I do a lot of business with them to this day.

At another time I was trying to promote some business with a firm that specialised in training salesmen, all bluff, competent fellows with plenty to say for themselves. The office contained about ten desks set out in two rows, and each man seated facing the door, one behind the other. As a green-horn, I would enter that office, my stomach in my shoes, to a sea of faces and a barrage of wisecracks, and it didn't help one bit to know they were all experts in salesmanship.

Some time later one of the men confided in me.

'We all really admired you, the way you used to bounce in and all of us baiting you so mercilessly.'

It came as an unexpected and pleasant surprise to know that as I stood quaking in my shoes and struck dumb with embarrassment, I was actually being admired!

Each time you encounter a difficult situation, look upon it as a valuable experience. Practice does make perfect. It is defeatist to opt out and deprive yourself of the chance to learn how to handle conflict, whether it is your own or other people's.

An Attitude of Mind

Speaking as someone who has had success as a saleswoman

but who has never taken a training course in her life, I admit I cannot judge if I would have fared better with instruction. This lack of training was not due to smugness but to the stark reality of always being too busy with the business. I suspect that most people are smart enough to see through obvious salesmanship anyway, and I have been told that my approach is refreshing.

Anyone, I mean *anyone*, who gets on reasonably well with people and who makes an effort to achieve empathy, can sell if;

- They accept that not everyone will be impressed.

- They accept rejection impersonally.

- They persevere until they do find someone to impress.

Perseverance

Look at it this way. You make five calls on potential customers, four show you the door and the fifth one is non-committal. Do you give up?

Not at all. You make a further call on the 'non-committed' case and 100 calls on other potential customers. Even if you fail to walk away with orders to break your competitors' hearts, you are sure to have left some doors open. Call again and eventually a percentage of this percentage will respond in some way.

People need to get used to other people and to feel secure with them.

Remember DETERMINATION.

Failure to make an Impression

It may be that those you are calling on are suspicious of new firms and new faces. Keep calling, so that you become a familiar and then a welcome visitor. Never stay too long in the beginning, as this may make them hostile. But do smile a lot. You may grow on them.

This is OPTIMISM, one of your most important weapons.

Accepting Rejection

The most common reason for rejection is that they are happy with their existing suppliers of your goods or service. Be philosophical about this one. When you have established your clientele, you would not like to believe that any Tom, Dick or Harriet could bowl into Purchasing and appropriate the business that would normally have come your way. By all means leave your card, so that they contact you if No. 1 Supplier commits some unforgivable sin, like charging them twice or forgetting the Chief Buyer's Christmas Bottle.

If the buyer informs you that his brother-in-law is currently supplying them with your products, forget it. You must accept lost causes with RESIGNATION and never allow wasted efforts from the past to cloud your aims for the future.

I truly believe that DETERMINATION, OPTIMISM AND RESIGNATION are compatible allies in your fight to the top.

The Shortest Route to Management

I also believe that learning to sell can be a marvellous opportunity to progress within your field, whether you are employed by a large company, striking out on your own in business, or employed in a smaller company where there is no established sales force.

In all these situations you are maintaining contact with the life-blood of the company, the clientele. Customers after all are responsible for paypackets. A salesperson who is on good terms with clients, or who is responsible for introducing new business, has a decided advantage.

Salespeople in larger companies who are worth their salt become Area Managers, then Departmental Managers and then possibly Directors. Self-employed business people increase their turnovers more rapidly. Those who work for smaller businesses should automatically find themselves highly placed in the hierarchy as their company grows and prospers.

To summarise, initiating new business is important because:

(a) As an employee, you will enjoy far greater powers of manipulation within your company with regard to the new business you have introduced than with existing contacts that have been handed to you, perhaps from a previous employee or from another overworked salesperson's area.
(b) If you decide to become self-employed, you will need to sell yourself and your products or service right from scratch.

The latter example would, of course, exclude salespeople who leave their previous employment taking a large percentage of the business with them. This is entirely a matter of personal ethics and may depend to a degree on any sense of grievance felt by the former employee towards that company.

I would like to add that I am neither condoning nor trying to justify such behaviour. Nevertheless it is a common occurrence, and it is up to employers to protect themselves as far as possible (see p. 117).

4

INITIATING NEW BUSINESS THROUGH PERSONAL CONTACT

If you wish to sell your product or service through personal contact, the first obvious step is to find your market (through yellow pages, advertisements in the paper, word of mouth or simply locating a likely venue in your area). Then you must do one of the following:

(a) Write for an appointment.
(b) Telephone for an appointment.
(c) Cold call.

Which method proves to be most successful for you depends to a degree on a combination of your personality type, the kind of business you are operating in and the desirability of what you are selling and how competitive your market.

Writing for an Appointment

If your company is well established, with an excellent reputation and all the prestige that goes with it, or if you are offering something unusual or new, then this is probably a good way to make contact.

You must word your letter carefully.

Point 1 – Catch the attention

Start on a positive note so that you catch your prospect's attention in the first sentence, otherwise he/she may not bother to finish reading it.

Point 2 – Hold the interest

Once you have your prospect's attention, you can explain your product or service in greater detail, emphasising its purpose/originality/effectiveness. Most people are intrigued by innovation.

Point 3 – Whet the appetite

Can you offer your prospect special terms or a special introductory offer? Can it be 'tailored' in some way so that it suits the company's needs?

Put a time limit on it though. Otherwise it may drift around the office and become forgotten. You're looking for business *now*.

Point 4 – Reassure your prospect

What else do you have to offer your prospect besides this terrific product/service? Be reassuring about your personal attention to detail, your back-up service, after-care, concern about quality or whatever else might be applicable.

If your prospect does not respond after a week or two, you could follow up with a telephone call.

'Good morning, Mrs Buykeen. This is Sally Smith of Creative Design Consultants. I wrote to you last week and I wondered if you had had a chance to consider our new concept for . . .?'

'I think that this is a good, respectful way to approach your prospect, since it accepts that a busy schedule may have prevented her from responding to your initial contact. Therefore if she has not properly assimilated the contents of your letter, you are leaving the options open by not putting her in a corner.

Then you can ring back next week.

Telephoning for an Appointment

If you are a saleswoman and you decide to telephone a buyer for an appointment (and in some cases a buyer may not see you unless you do), your manner may make or break you. It is amazing how many callers arouse hostility immediately they make contact with their prospect.

The wrong way

'Hi, Barry, this is Marie. My company makes XYZ products and I'll be in your area 10 o'clock on Tuesday. I'll pop in then and show you our super new range.'

Point 1 – 'Hi Barry.' Barry thinks: who the hell are you? This racy style of using Christian names to all and sundry, even to people to whom one is speaking for the first time, may be successful in some instances, but most people tend to be suspicious, and rightly so. Over-familiarity is off-putting and distancing. The minority who would be unruffled by this approach would not in any case be upset by formality, even if they found it a little quaint.

Point 2 – 'I'll be in your area 10 o'clock on Tuesday.' Barry thinks: hard luck, I'm golfing Tuesday! (At this stage he may voice his reaction, in which case for golfing read 'in conference'.)

What an insult! You are dictating to this high powered, hard pressed executive on whom you wish to unload 10,000 of your XYZ products when it would be convenient for you to pay a call on him. Well, maybe he isn't especially high powered and hard pressed, but what do you know about his self-image? Take the trouble to find out what is acceptable to him and then make the effort to accommodate him.

Point 3 – 'Show you our super new range.' Barry's next reaction is unprintable.

Dispense with the overstatements. How is your product going to help him? That is what he is interested in.

The right way

'Good afternoon, Mr Body. My name is Marie Mason of Jones, Jenkins and Partners. We are manufacturers of XYZ and we feel we could offer quality and service to your company. I'd like to ask if you would grant me an interview. Would Tuesday be all right? What time?'

There is room for modification here. Use the words that come naturally to you. They will sound fine if you remember that you are asking Barry Body a favour and that he is entitled to respect and consideration.

Of course the respect and consideration angle is not always a two-way affair. I heard an interesting little story about an agency canvasser telephoning firms in order to promote their secretarial staff. A young lady got through to her prospect and started off brightly with her pre-rehearsed speech, to be cut short by a curt 'Fuck off'.

Visibly shaken, she replaced the receiver.

'Get back to him immediately,' was her boss's stern command.

'I can't,' she whispered, horrified.

'You can and you must. He's not getting away with that.'

So she did. 'Oh, hello, Mr Body,' she said, 'I believe we were cut off.'

He laughed, amazed and impressed.

'Well, you've certainly got some guts,' he said. 'What can I do for you?'

Cold-calling

Cold-calling is a business term for an unannounced visit by an unknown party. It is a method that many people dislike, although it is one of my own favourite methods of selling.

In a competitive industry where you are possibly rather small fry the methods of writing in or telephoning do not always work so well. A letter gives a buyer time to think of many good reasons he/she should not see you (since it is going to be just one of many all the same), and that is assuming it was not consigned to the waste-tub unread, with all the others. A telephone call may be more successful, but once again, although your prospect may not be particularly busy when you call, a future firm commitment may not be convenient or desirable. (Why should I see another blasted rep – our shipping order might come in tomorrow.)

On the other hand, if you call, and providing you are not shown the door too forcibly by his secretary, you *keep* calling, eventually you may wheedle your way in.

Admittedly cold-calling can be a complete waste of time, sometimes demoralising, often mentally exhausting, but you should get to see a fair proportion of the people you call on. While you are waiting hopefully in Reception, your buyer may make a snap decision that he/she can spare you a moment before rushing off to lunch with the boss.

But first you must deal with the receptionist

Most companies rely on the Receptionist to sort out the desirable from the undesirable visitors. As a newcomer, do not delude yourself into believing you do not come into the latter classification. There are two basic types of Receptionist:

(a) Those who would like to help you.

(b) Those who would not like to help you.

Whether or not she appears to be a dragon lady, approach

[31]

her in a friendly manner with your request that she asks the buyer to spare you a moment. Try to put the right words into her mouth by the careful choice of your own words.

Unless the wanted party has specifically requested not to be disturbed, or is engaged, she has no choice but to announce your arrival. How she does so may influence the success or failure of your call.

Hand her your business card so that she gets your name and service right when announcing you.

If you are unlucky and in spite of your efforts you find you are dealing with a negative or hostile attitude, try not to visibly cringe as her dulcet tones reverberate into the mouthpiece.

'Someone to see you, Mr Body. I said you were busy. About what? 'Ang on a mo, uhmmmmm . . .'

Your buyer may see you anyway. If not, call again.

At the Interview

You will probably stand or fall on how deftly you handle this first important interview. If you stumble a little, it does not necessarily mean curtains for you, but do try to have a few answers at your fingertips. You want your buyer to see you again, but not just as a pleasant distraction to brighten a dull day.

Your buyer may see you personally, or may send his or her secretary to check you out first. Since the chances are that the secretary is handling most of the routine office work anyway, treat her (or him) exactly as if she were your buyer. Even if she does not play an active part in making decisions, she probably has considerable influence in the running of the office.

'Good morning. Thank you for seeing me. I won't take up too much of your time, but I'd like to introduce myself. I'm . . . of . . .' Hand over your business card and literature, explain about service, offers, deliveries, discounts, etc., then play it by ear.

[32]

Never prolong this first interview unless it is apparent that your buyer (or the secretary) is interested and wants to chat. It is the most critical meeting you will have. Further contact depends on its success. If your prospect cannot get rid of you, there may not be any further meetings.

Unless your prospect immediately takes a personal interest in you, stick strictly to business. There will be time to get better acquainted in the course of the successful business dealings which are perhaps ahead of you.

One final point. Until you know and relate to your buyer very well, or unless you have been summoned, never, never call at 4.10 on Friday afternoon!

Flattery

If you wish to indulge a business associate with a token of approval, remember that overdoing flattery undervalues it. Keep it subtle, low-key, slightly indirect.

If a business executive tells you about winning some particular point at a meeting or with an opponent, don't gasp in admiration. Murmur casually, 'You don't let anyone take advantage of you, do you, Mr B!'

He'll interpret your meaning without feeling patronised, and you have acknowledged his skills without being too effusive.

5

YOUR IMAGE – DON'T UNDER-RATE YOURSELF

Once I had to arrange for some photosetting to be done and I was introduced by a mutual acquaintance to an associate of his in that field. For the purposes of this anecdote I shall call this associate Jim.

'My company is just down the road', said Jim grandly. He took me there and introduced me to the 'staff', then conducted me on a tour of all the equipment and machines. Suitably impressed, I made the appropriate admiring noises and the company and I proceeded to do business.

This went on for many weeks. Jim's staff was composed of three smart and efficient middle-aged ladies, and they and I got on extremely well.

Suddenly Jim wasn't around anymore.

'Where's Jim these days?' I enquired of Sally.

Sally, chic, pleasant and normally unassuming, handed me the quotation she had just completed for setting my client's service manual. 'He's not here any more,' she replied.

'So who's taken over the business?' I asked innocently.

'I beg your pardon?' said Sally, rather too quickly, raising her carefully plucked eyebrows.

'Has he sold out and gone on to pastures new?'

Was my face red when Sally, with a few choice expletives betraying a dangerous element to her nature I had not previously suspected, put me roundly in the picture.

Jim didn't own the typesetting agency.

Sally did.

Jim wasn't even employed by the typesetting agency. He was merely a freelancer, something of a parasite, for he liked to use Sally's premises as a business address. Sally was a generous type and didn't mind, but she was furious to discover how he had deliberately stolen her thunder, for Sally owned the typesetting agency, the shop premises, all the equipment and machines, and she alone was responsible for paying the staff.

It was not even necessary for Jim to hoodwink me. I dealt directly with the agency and he was not paid commission. He just wanted to be a big wheel. He was a poseur.

That's the main problem. Men tend to over-rate themselves, although maybe not all are such extreme cases as Jim.

And women under-rate themselves. For wasn't Sally just as much to blame for my mistake as Jim? Because while Jim was shouting his mouth off, there was Sally, quiet, unassuming, industrious, tapping away at her setter. I had come to the obvious, if not the most intelligent, conclusion. Women should stop colluding in allowing these men to prolong their egoistic fantasies at women's expense.

In respect of her own business life a woman client of mine believes in blowing one's own trumpet, loudly and clearly, so that even the thickest ear can assimilate.

'How do you enjoy your status as a businesswoman?' I once asked her.

'I find men are frightened of me, I really do,' she stated, and then added wickedly and with brutal honesty, 'And I must say I derive a great deal of pleasure out of this.'

Little wonder they are frightened!

Take the typewriter rep, just a little too cocksure for her liking. 'I'm the good-looking one,' he smarmed on being introduced for the first time. Thereafter my client addressed him as 'Good-looking' whenever he called, and watched him getting madder and madder and madder . . . The tables were turned and he just could not cope.

Of course, you cannot adopt this manner with anyone you

[35]

wish to impress, any more than you would call on a client with the announcement, 'I'm the gorgeous one'. But if you are pretty, make the most of it. Make the most of all of your assets.

Men do, fairly or unfairly.

If it was socially acceptable for men to weep to get their own way, you can bet your life there would be wet hankies all over the place. For women, the shedding of a few tears in times of dire emergency might be a useful ruse, but it is not something to be used indiscriminately. The guilt feelings it arouses may easily turn against you.

Invoking pity in this way could never be part of my image, and I would not use it under any circumstances. At the same time, I cannot see that it is any more reprehensible than the use of aggression, emotional blackmail or lies, all of which are methods of manipulation frequently used by men.

Be Yourself

This might sound like a contradiction in the light of my previous comments, but I can assure you it is not. Image is one thing, personality another and both should complement each other. Image is to do with self-projection, self-confidence, self-preservation. Personality is what makes you tick, deep down inside. Soft-spoken gentle people can be just as successful as fast-talking extroverts with lots of funny stories up their sleeves. And both can project an image which inspires confidence, authority and empathy in those with whom they communicate.

In essence, be yourself, but be sure to project an image that does you justice and fits in with your ambitions.

[36]

Dress to Succeed

'Dress is an area where a lot of women let themselves down,' says Anne Watts of National Westminster Bank. 'If you have no dress, colour or style sense, why not head for one of the companies who can help you?' (e.g. Wardrobe, House of Colour, etc.).

Deryn Stewart, Area Manager for Wedgwood Hotel Ware, endorses Anne's statement. 'You must be immaculate at all times, polished nails, perfect make-up and hair, especially when you are in contact with clients. It is more expected of a woman than it is of a man. It seems to me a man can get away with having a night on the town and turning up for work looking slightly scruffy.'

I shall, however, leave the last word to Maggie of Warlingham.

'A small shop like mine, offering a personal service, is much better for the customer, especially the problem customer. After all, if I make a mistake in advising a customer, I have to look at this mistake until the clothes wear out!

'Basically, one is always striving for perfection. I know it's not a perfect world, but still we aim for perfection. It is something to live up to.'

Maggie is Irish, a dark and statuesque lady. She moves like a model because that is what she is. She started modelling in 1958 when she was chosen by Norman Hartnell to 'do' his collection when he was on tour in Belfast.

From there, her career 'snowballed'. She modelled in Dubai and Berlin, both for manufacturers and for exhibitions. Twenty years later, she is still modelling for catalogues.

'I model for the larger lady, sizes 16 to 26. You see, they can't get bodies like mine these days; they seem to specialise in sizes 12 to 16. You just can't put the same designs on the larger figure. As ladies get older, rounder, they need a different kind of merchandise. It's like painting a beautiful picture, signing it "Rembrandt".'

Maggie is proud of her signature and rightly so. 'Dressed by

Maggie' is undoubtedly a status symbol in these parts.

Soon she would be off to Finland to collect some of their 'beautiful cottons' for her shop.

'I could make a completely new person of you,' remarked Maggie, eyeing my chain-store sweater and the skirt I inherited from my friend after she lost weight.

I admit I could be tempted. . . .

A few small points about images:

(a) If you are in a serious business, project yourself so that you are taken seriously. You would not expect a brain surgeon to operate on you in a pair of cut-down jeans or a kaftan.

(b) Never wear your pleb T-shirt with I'VE BEEN TO MALTA in big red capitals across the chest. No, not even shopping in Sainsbury's. (You never know who you might bump into in Sainsbury's!)

(c) If you are in a creative field, you can be more outrageous in the way you dress without hindrance to your success. People quite expect artists to wear ancient jeans and sloppy sweaters. If you are in the pop business, it's generally OK to hulk around in black leather and pink hair.

(d) Your demeanour! Happy people are always a tonic to have around, except maybe first thing Monday morning.

(e) If your dog has just died, keep it to yourself.

Just one final point about non-conformist creative people. Never allow your lack of conformity in appearance to extend to your behaviour, as did one artist I know, who entered his prospect's office, said 'Hi' and unceremoniously proceeded to settle himself unasked into her chair and put his feet up on her desk.

Her reaction? 'Bloody cheek! He's not getting any business from me.'

6

BOSSES AND BUYERS

The term 'boss' may include both your immediate boss and those in the hierarchy above who have, or may have in the future, influence over your progression within the company. The term 'buyer' refers to any client of your company with whom you deal either by telephone or personal visit on behalf of your company and whose goodwill could be instrumental in your future progress.

I will not make any excuse for linking these two categories together. They are often interchangeable. I have always been amused when the uninitiated remark, 'Aren't you lucky not to be answerable to a boss!' Well, let me tell you that at any time I have over 100 bosses. My clients!

I concede that when you run your own business you have more control, cannot be sacked, cannot be forced to operate in a way not to your liking. All the same, if worth cultivating, your buyer will always call the shots, even though the negotiations appear to be on an equal footing. If you give good service, your buyer won't want to upset you, but never forget that buyers are responsible for paypackets at the end of the month.

As for bosses, they are buyers too. Don't forget that *selling is the shortest route to management.* So start off by getting your boss to buy your ideas, your talents, your expertise. Then, maybe, he will give you a chance to try out your skills on the customers.

Prove your worth. If your efforts are not appreciated, accepted and rewarded, you still have something to sell to a more progressive company – *experience*.

It is kinder to your personal stress threshold always to get your experience first, consolidate your position and attack from strength.

I would like now to tell you about some different kinds of buyers and bosses. Some may seem a little larger than life, but I promise you that I have met them all.

For the purpose of this section I have dropped the clumsy 'he/she' and the impersonal 'they' and trust you will accept that I do not intend to be 'sexist'. Far from it. But for a lighthearted examination of real-life personalities, it seems more natural and appropriate to use the individual gender as it first comes to mind.

The Professional

The Professional, be it man or woman, is primarily looking out for the company. If you can prove that you are good for the company, then she will be good for you. As your boss or buyer, she is not fickle. As a boss, she will permit you to update old systems and make other changes around the office. Considering her as your buyer, you must gradually build up her confidence in you and your ability to handle her work and woo her away from existing suppliers and services.

She will deal with you pleasantly and concisely and co-operate when things go wrong, as they occasionally do, without malice of temperament. Once she is satisfied, she will not desert you without good reason.

Handling. Never give her good reason to alter her good opinion of you.

The Self-Employed Man or Woman

He is busy and grateful for someone to deal with his requirements with a minimum of fuss. He'll be uninterested in details unless they are relevant.

Handling. Never keep him chatting. He is under pressure, like you. If he is your buyer, don't worry, he is far too preoccupied to see both you *and* your competitors.

If he is your boss, try to be sympathetic to his problems and only disturb him when it's really important (e.g. when it's time you had a rise!).

The Prima Donna

The Prima Donna is sensitive about her position. She feels precarious, for she was once just a clerk and now she has taken exams in her chosen field and qualified. She has the added responsibility of being in charge of the female staff and they, for the most part, resent her. (Sex discrimination is not, of course, confined to men.)

She has earned her stripes but has to keep proving herself, contending with envy from the women and a patronising attitude from the men.

Handling. Whether she is your buyer or your boss, and providing she is not too unbearable, treat her with respect, which will endear you to her. She isn't a dragon. Just misunderstood. Maybe all she really needs is an ally.

The Whizzkid

Young and dynamic, he'll pace the floor, treating his audience (you!) to bursts of a rhetoric bearing more relation to the projection of his personality than to the point in question. His name is probably Simon or Dermot. He always carries a Filo-fax and has his initials embossed in gold leaf on his briefcase.

The Whizzkid, as his name presupposes, gets things done. They may get done right. They may get done wrong. But they do most definitely get done.

He is urgency personified and does not recognise the word 'impossible', whether relating to overtime or the fact that you cannot get his order to him tomorrow as the parts are still in Coventry and waiting to be screwed together.

The Whizzkid may make advances towards you, just like the sexual opportunist. However, while the more common latter species sees such a sinister little set-up as a straight exchange (his co-operation for your body), the mind of the Whizzkid operates quite differently. He will consider that he is bestowing his favours upon fortunate *you*, a bonus to supplement any benefit or business he puts your way.

Handling. Providing he does not lose face, the rejection of his advances does not necessarily preclude you from working for him or transacting business with him, assuming that you can take the pace. Tact in dealing with the inevitable amazement that will ensue after your refusal of his splendid offer will be the key to your success.

The Mentor

This can be a most satisfying business relationship, mutually rewarding and perhaps developed with an older person of the professional type who is well established. He will enjoy acting as mentor and will occasionally criticise your eye make-up.

A busy man, he will be pleased to know he can rely on your integrity, and his company will benefit, for you will hate to let him down on a promise or fail to sort out a problem.

Handling. Deal with him naturally. There is no need for subterfuge.

The Waverer

The Waverer is a very difficult customer (or boss) indeed. He will insist that he will know what he wants when he sees it, but cannot be specific about any aspect of his requirements.

This will be a guessing game.

The Waverer can also be pernickety, splitting hairs, fussing, changing and cancelling. Therefore much time will be expended on false errands, pointless research and unnecessary investigations. Eventually he will probably settle on whatever it was you suggested in the first place. Finally, he will decide that he doesn't like it, but this will only occur 2 months after the event.

After all this, if you're lucky, you may have accrued sufficient profit to pay for your parking meter. That is, providing you didn't get a ticket while he was busy not making up his mind.

Handling. If he is your buyer, ditch him if you can. He is more trouble than he is worth. However, if it is not politic for you to do this, try to pin him down and make him put his instructions in writing. If a meeting is of great importance, take along an associate. You may need a witness!

If he's your boss, couldn't you apply for a transfer to another department? Obviously it would not promote your cause to run him down to his superiors, but you could express a sudden deep desire to 'work in Personnel' and maybe even elevate your position.

The Poker Face

Inscrutable, offhand, he will not indicate whether you're wanted or not. He is never rude, nor actually unpleasant, but he gives no indication of whether he is impressed or bored.

Perhaps he is wary of dealing with women, but this may not be entirely due to male chauvinism, especially if your business takes you into the realms of what was formerly an exclusively male bastion. It could be normal human mistrust of the unexpected – as you might feel, say, coming across a male attendant in the Ladies' Loo.

If you become an expert in ballistic missiles, you must expect some slight hint of unease. Give him a chance.

Handling. Most of all, don't try too hard, and don't be intimidated or offended while he is adjusting. Never over-compensate by attempting to blind him with science.

In my experience people who hold a little in reserve at first often make more lasting relationships, in business or outside it. Your intention is, after all, to instil faith in your ability, not just to convince him what an ardent feminist you are, however admirable that may be.

The Easy Woman or Man

A false sense of security is induced by her easy unconcern. 'I'll leave it to you', she says, 'you know what I mean. Yes, blue would be OK, but if that's difficult, whatever you can get hold of. No, I'm not sure about the size, like this (gesticulating) and like that. Can we have it next week?'

Do not be fooled. Either she will send it back or demand a ridiculously high discount because it's wrong.

Handling. Be hard. Set it out in writing and make her sign. It's a matter of self-preservation to be hard with the Easy Woman.

The Foreigner

Foreigners are of course as different from each other as we British and their personalities may fit into any of the aforementioned groups. However, they may have certain foibles peculiar to their own race and creed.

For instance, you need not feel vastly insulted if a Middle Eastern gentleman offers you a £10 tip for an exceptional piece of organisation on his behalf. It could be a sincere mark of appreciation, and, if he is insistent and has behaved well towards you, may even be graciously accepted. Unless he is also a sexual opportunist, there are no strings attached.

Handling. So before making assumptions, do make allowances for their culture. It may even teach you a thing or two.

The Secretary/PA

Frequently in smaller companies the buying of such items as stationery, office equipment, printing, technical drawing products, canteen foods and allied business services is left to the discretion of the senior secretaries. Therefore, although this category does not come under the 'boss' definition, I think it is useful to include it as a strong buying entity.

Whilst conceding that the title 'secretary' is hardly typical of one type of person, this group does have aspects common to all. The most important is that they are secretaries, not professional buyers. Therefore, they are unlikely to be as knowledgeable on the product or service you offer, or the technicalities of dealing with suppliers, as an experienced buyer. This makes them vulnerable to backlash through no fault of their own and may result in their being timid buyers. This may manifest itself in pathetically small orders, split packs, sudden urgent requests before 'the boss finds out that I forgot'.

Handling. Treat your secretary/buyer with understanding and co-operation. When she gets it wrong, help her out, and together you may progress to greater things. She may put in a good word for you with the boss, which may result in a worthwhile deal. She may even fill his shoes one day.

In any case helping people to get things right must be the greatest source of job satisfaction . . . next to money!

The Thoroughly Nasty Piece of Work

You just can't please some people. If your boss or buyer is totally unbearable, despite your efforts at tact, kindness, understanding, firmness and careful assertiveness, and the only course seems to be complete self-effacement, then think again.

Being constantly conciliatory is not good for one's own self-esteem.

Handling. It is a difficult one.

Some women might cope by 'giving as good as they get'. Others might feel it was like 'sinking down to someone else's level', and decide it was more appropriate to find a new job rather than work for a boss like this.

If your company is a large one, perhaps you could go to Personnel and ask them if they can effect a transfer for you to another department. They are probably aware of his shortcomings, since you are probably his fourth secretary since Christmas, and they should be sympathetic.

If the Nasty Piece of Work is your buyer, then it might be possible to deal with him mostly by letter and telephone, in both cases trying to keep communication short, businesslike and to the point.

The Hell Raiser

Any Hell Raiser is firmly convinced that the louder he shouts, the more right he is. Unless you have extremely good lungs, it is impossible to compete. There is little point anyway. In his present condition he is oblivious to any views you may have.

This category is rather different from the 'Nasty Piece of Work', who goes out of his way to be unpleasant. The Hell Raiser is at this moment 'out of control', and he is angry with *you*.

Handling. The only course of action is to keep quiet until he has let off all his steam and collapsed, exhausted, his head in his hands. Then ask quiet, respectful questions as to how, why, when and what and fix your eyes on him intently as if the whole world depends on his responses.

This will deflate his anger and simultaneously enable you to ascertain exactly what went wrong. Above all, control the impulse to indulge in retaliatory remarks.

At best, he may eventually feel bad enough to apologise for his ill-temper. At worst, you will take the credit for being the unruffled businesslike woman you always intended to be.

If there is some justification for his attack on you, you can quietly apologise. If not, you could murmur, 'I'm very upset that you feel this way . . .'

There is no loss of face in behaving in a respectable, civilised manner, and it has nothing to do with your sex. A man would gain respect by exactly the same technique.

7

LUNCHING YOUR CLIENT

An invitation to lunch will be generally well received by your client as a compliment to his or her importance and standing with your company. Find out what food your client prefers and if he or she has any favourite haunts among the local eating places.

If it is a popular restaurant, be sure to book a table. Nothing is more humiliating than to arrive at your destination in anticipation of a tasty meal, with wine and all the trimmings, only to find the last table was taken 5 minutes ago. The subsequent panic, hurried consultations and dashes around town, even if successful, will ensure that client will never forget that lunch date.

Your Male Client

When it comes to settling the bill, some men are quite tickled at being taken out and paid for. Others, particularly older men, may still be old-fashioned enough to flap around feeling emasculated, and embarrassing both of you.

If you are an executive business lady with an established company behind you, it's easy enough to say, 'Don't worry, the company's paying'. However, if you are self-employed or newly set up, this may not console him.

Just tell him it is a business lunch and he is your guest and leave it at that. The more matter of fact you are about it, the less strange it will seem. If you allow him to make you feel uncomfortable too, it will only compound the problem.

When the waiter plants the bill squarely in front of your client (they always do, don't they), pause a second until he (the waiter) turns his back, then slide it neatly across the table towards you. Make out the cheque, then push bill and cheque, face down, back to the centre of the table.

If your client is a particularly bad case, it is more discreet if you have previously positioned the wine basket and pepper mill between you, a little towards your side of the table, thus shielding your action in writing the cheque and sparing him the discomfort of accidentally noticing that there are two sevens in the left-hand box of the total column.

Your Female Client

It can be almost as difficult treating your female client to lunch, as many women try to insist on going dutch with other women, even in respect of business lunches. If she does, of course you must refuse. She may then make a big thing about it being her turn next time. Just smile and change the subject.

The Advantages of the Business Lunch

A business lunch is a useful tool, for gaining information, for cementing the relationship with your client and acting as a form of insurance. After such a cosy tête-à-tête your competitors won't stand much chance, at least not for a while.

You can get to know your client personally out of the office environment, discuss leisure pursuits, find out whether the character reading for their star sign is accurate (everyone loves astrology and talking about themselves) and discover their hopes and dreams for the future. You can also get a little confidential about yourself. In other words, you can promote a friendly relationship which can only make your future business dealings with your client more pleasant and more profitable.

8

GO IT ALONE AND
BECOME A SELF-MADE
WOMAN

'If only I could do what you do! If only I could start up my own business, but . . .'

These are the words that inspired this book. I can't help thinking that if I had £1 for every female employee who has wistfully uttered these words to me, I would be a rich woman by now.

Of course the more determined among us are inevitably finding a niche for ourselves in the business market, and are without doubt a force to be reckoned with. High-powered women seem to prosper mostly in major towns and cities where attitudes are more up-to-date and more flexible, and where, possibly, women are encouraged to have a better opinion of themselves. For some years they have tended to stick to certain areas – those areas in which women already had some experience – e.g. the beauty industry, employment agencies and boutiques.

This is already changing, for women are learning to become mechanics, fork-lift truck drivers and plumbers. Why shouldn't a good female mechanic run her own motor repair workshop in much the same way as a good secretary, skilled with people, might start up her own employment agency, or a reader in a publishing company her own literary agency?

The permutations are endless.

Not so long ago I was visited by two young unemployed women. They wanted to clean my windows; they were starting up their own window-cleaning round.

These young entrepreneurs dreamed of success in much the same way as any other financially astute woman. When they had got some capital behind them and a name for themselves, they were going to go all out for big office-cleaning contracts. Eventually they would employ others to carry out the work while they had lunch with their contacts, doing deals and directing operations from their lush West End offices.

I hope they make it. They have a long way to go and a lot of hard work to do, but if a man can do it, why can't they?

'If only I could do what you do, but . . .'

What I shall now attempt to do is to eliminate the 'buts'. 'But' must be the most negative word in the English language.

As an old hand I think I am well qualified to describe exactly what it is like to be your own boss – and other people's. I am also well aware of all the pitfalls you are likely to come up against.

Like men!

And even other women . . .

Prejudice

More years ago than I care to remember, when women drivers ceased to be regarded as objects of wonder and took to the road en masse, men called us 'silly cows' and made statements like 'Keep off the road today, the wife's driving'. Some of us developed a complex and consequently lacked confidence.

But as we gained experience, we discovered that men are not more skilled than we, but less inhibited because they do not feel a need to justify themselves. (Have you ever noticed how a man will risk his neck to overtake you on a two-lane carriageway at 80 mph and then turn right?)

Business is, even today, a bit like that. At the moment men

still hold the upper hand, but slowly it will change, despite similar preconceived notions.

Someone once said that there is no sentiment in business. But business is to do with people and people are often sentimental as well as awkward, tolerant, devious, kind, mean and unpredictable. We are all products of our own backgrounds, experiences and personal prejudices.

As a woman making out in business therefore, you may be susceptible to prejudice. Join the club. To a greater or lesser extent, so are cockneys, coloured people, ginger-haired people, lapsed freemasons, very short people, atheists and many, many more. It isn't fair, but that's how it is. Occasionally you may even benefit as some people tend to over-compensate to assuage their guilt.

It helps if you are not intimidated by over-confidence or aggression. Whenever you stall, ignore the irate blasts, shrug your shoulders and carry on as if nothing had happened. If you have the ability to laugh at yourself, or can conduct yourself with panache in harassing situations, you are on the road to confidence and autonomy.

All things considered, you would still like to go into business for yourself. Whatever enterprise you envisage, you must sell yourself and learn to contend with all the complications that arise.

Freelance during your holidays, or, if you can, find a job that will give you the insight you need. Find out first hand what it is all about and what makes *you* tick.

Treat with caution people who say, 'You could easily start up on your own with your flair and personality'. They may be right, but their judgment may be superficial. Energy, the ability to converse and a forthright manner may be assets, but greater perception is needed to see what really counts when going it alone.

THE COMPETITIVE WOMAN

A Personal Philosophy

As in almost anything worthwhile, you have to descend in order to rise higher. Could you start at the bottom, maybe for a second time? Could you cope with being vulnerable? Could you look upon it all as character-building, a learning process, a kind of army square-bashing? Even when you have to paint the coal white?

Inner Strength

A situation most calculated to dent a new salesman's ego happened to an associate of mine. (It happens to men too.) One of his first calls was on a buyer who especially prided himself on his own knowledge and experience. After the salesman left, the buyer telephoned the poor chap's firm. 'Don't send him to me again, wasting my time. He knows absolutely nothing.'

That buyer forgot that he was not himself born with knowledge and experience. No doubt, if he could, he would have taken out a patent on it.

Accept that you will come across people like this, jealous of their positions and loath to allow you to join the club. Draw upon your inner strength and never let other people's opinions of you shake your resolve and your confidence in your ability.

A High 'Aggro' Tolerance Level

This is imperative. I have sometimes felt severely hassled by just about every client on my books. If I had reacted unfavourably towards them each time I got annoyed, I would now be out of business.

Jobs for the Girls

Although I have devoted a chapter in this book to Employing Staff (Chapter 21), I feel it is relevant to comment about the pitfalls for self-made women who employ their friends, relatives and neighbours.

There is always a tendency to cling to what is familiar when one is first starting out on a strange and perhaps frightening new project. But be prepared for the pitfalls before deciding to take on any of the following.

Your friend

She may be a super and loyal friend and efficient in her own right. But just as you are familiar with her, so is she with you.

There will be no barrier, that necessary quota of reserve that will occur with a stranger. She is accustomed to you and may unwittingly take advantage of you. What may be of tremendous importance to you may be of no consequence to her, and she may not be unduly worried about the results of her actions.

For instance, suppose you employ your friend to take care of the office while you are out on business. Will you return unexpectedly to the office to find the telephone unattended because she's dashed off to minister to her sick boy friend? She may be right when she says, 'They can always call back later', but I doubt it. Most callers would probably decide you were rather a poor lot and contact your competitor, whose staff would not dream of leaving their posts for fear of losing their jobs.

Friends may also bring their emotional problems to work, losing both of you valuable time.

When employing staff, you must start exactly as you mean to go on, but with a friend you may be too far along the path of familiarity to establish the right direction.

[55]

Your family

Most of the above points also may apply to family, unless they are direct beneficiaries and jointly shouldering their responsibilities. However, tolerance levels tend to be easier among close family, and disputes discussed more readily and openly, which can make a lot of difference to the smooth running of the operation.

Your neighbour

Never, repeat never, employ anyone who lives within spitting distance of your home. This person may be pleasant and sufficiently new to you not to encompass the kinds of problems which occur when employing friends, but just supposing she's . . .

(a) Not as bright as you thought she was.

(b) The street busybody.

(c) Indispensable to her husband and children (Don't forget that they are are within spitting distance too.)

Do you know for certain she might not be one or more of these things, and are you positive you might not prefer at some time to dispense with her services? How will you feel stepping out into your garden to water your begonias before dashing back to the office, only to meet her accusing stare over the garden fence.

Unless you are extremely thick-skinned, or very, very sure of your personal judgment, employ your neighbour at your peril.

Start Slowly

Finally, do acquaint yourself with Parkinson's Law, which is the notion that work expands to fill the time allotted to it.

For economy's sake, start with part-time employees and do not allow their hours to extend until it is practical to do so. As the workload increases, it is probably better to have a few part-timers than one full-time employee. This means you will never be left 'in the lurch' due to sickness, holidays or termination or employment.

Of course not all businesses operate in the same way and some require continuity more than others. In this case there may be little choice.

When One Door Closes

My first major onslaught on the world of commerce took me to the city several years ago, where I started at the top of a building housing numerous small businesses. (You always start at the top; it's easier on the legs to take the lift up and then work your way down quickly, floor by floor, via the stairs.) I called on each company with a stunted little speech and a price list. After 2 weeks of repeat calls to the more amenable buyers, I then secured just one client.

This company now no longer deals with me, as my buyer left and the man who took his place refused absolutely to see me. I don't know why. Maybe he disapproved of women in business.

FAILURE? Not a bit of it!

In the meantime, my service had been recommended to their larger associate company, which subsequently became one of my most profitable accounts and even exported some of my goods behind the Iron Curtain.

This is part of the joy of being in business. You never know what is around the corner.

The 'Plum' turns up when least expected.

Be ready for it!

9

CHEAP ENTERPRISE

You know you can run a business and are ready, mentally, to take the plunge. What is preventing you from taking that first step?

Lack of funding?

I would not deny that money helps a lot, but it is not conditional. Many people with nothing but a knack make it successfully to the top. It just takes a little longer. Lack of funding can be compensated for by patience and staying power.

The Pauper's Approach to Starting in Business

Start gradually

Could you afford to survive by working part-time leaving the remainder of each day free to explore the feasibility of your idea? There are several areas where part-time work is still available, in spite of the unemployment problem. They include typing, book-keeping, driving, market research, bar work, waiting, school administration.

You will need an answerphone, but there are some good, cheap systems on the market these days. (No doubt you will learn to live with the giggles, laughing boxes and other practical jokes until the novelty wears off among your circle of friends.) Work will extend to evenings and weekends, but if you are strong, healthy, totally absorbed in your project and sensible about taking some relaxation occasionally, you will thrive on this.

How will you know when to take the final plunge? The following indicators will be sufficient:

1 You have stopped biting your fingernails worrying about where the next order is coming from. However, you have started tearing your hair with frustration because there are not enough hours in the day.

2 Your bank manager has asked you to lunch.

3 You lost out on a deal because there was no space left on the tape in your answerphone. You need a secretary.

Get a loan

Banks and finance companies will be cautious about lending you money if you have no proven record of successful past business transactions with them. Alternatively, maybe you could find a sleeping partner, someone prepared to put cash up front for an interest and allow you to operate the business. In this instance be sure to consult a solicitor before committing yourself to anything, and have him draft up a mutually satisfactory agreement.

Personally I would not wish to take on a sleeping partner, preferring a free hand long-term, but this is a matter of choice.

Some people jump in at the deep end

If you have sufficient savings at least to support yourself for a few months and can obtain credit from your suppliers, this all or nothing approach may work, although considering it is risky. You would require several weeks to acquire and start processing your valuable orders. Unless yours is a cash on supply business, you will experience the added problems of getting in your money. Normally debtors should pay at the end of the month following the month of invoice, but many will keep you waiting longer.

Before you 'jump', work out all the pros and cons and don't do it unless:

1 You qualify for Government help (contact the Department of Employment for your free booklet outlining same).

2 You are very, very sure of yourself (enquire about NAT-WEST Starter Pack).

Obtaining credit

Whatever course you choose to get started, sooner or later you will realise that you cannot do justice to your idea without some help. You need credit. Let's face it, most business is conducted on credit. All big business is conducted on credit. Obtaining credit is another matter and an area in which some women appear to feel victimised.

Before you screw yourself up because you feel you are not treated seriously when approaching a company for credit, consider the following, and don't become over-sensitive in spite of some bad experiences.

Any company will be cautious before granting credit to a new enterprise, be it run by male or female. Any company likes to know it stands a fair chance of being paid. Do not take it as a personal insult that your proposed creditor requires two trade references and one from the bank.

Businesses go into liquidation every day through mis-management, overspending, negligence or plain bad luck. So how do you get all these references if you cannot get credit in the first place? It may seem like a Catch 22 situation, but there are procedures.

If you are starting your business gradually, freelance or possibly on the side in conjunction with something else, your first needs will be small anyway. Pay the first couple of orders on proforma invoices (i.e. invoices issued *before* supply of goods instead of after); then you will probably find you can request your next order on credit, providing it is fairly modest.

You should find you can build up your suppliers' confidence gradually in this way. If you encounter any difficulty, try the following.

Telephone your supplier and explain that although you are not an account customer, you need this consignment urgently. Could they possibly deliver tomorrow, although there obviously won't be time to clear your cheque?

If they are hesitant, you could try stepping up the pressure. Could the goods conceivably represent a missing link in your client's production schedule, thereby bringing machinery and work force to a total halt? Use your imagination.

Alternatively, you may know someone who would supply you initially on trust and who would give you credit. Use him for a while, pay his bills on time, and then ask him to act as your referee when you wish to gain credit from another party.

It should not be too difficult getting the ball rolling. As with most situations, it gets easier as you go along.

My first printer knew me personally and I dealt with him for a while. When I decided to go into the office equipment field, I approached a large wholesaler with a request to open an account. I had only one trade reference instead of the required two and had only been dealing with my bank for a few months. I poured out my apparently insurmountable problems to the credit controller, who was most sympathetic and granted me sizeable credit, despite my single trade reference and the cautious letter from my bank.

Later he was dismissed for embezzling company funds. What moral can be drawn from this I do not know.

Conversely, I once went into a large showroom to purchase a 1-ton delivery van for my business. The salesman laughed at me in derisive disbelief. He lost a sale.

[61]

Unfortunately there will always be offensive people in the world, ready to exploit inexperience, naivety or lack of confidence. They suffer from their own private complexes. If you cannot cope with them, then you are not cut out for business.

Money-saving Ideas for the New Entrepreneur

- Instead of paying a sizeable sum to have your first 100 sets of two-part numbered invoices printed, buy a duplicate book and ask your stationer to supply you with a rubber stamp of your name, address and telephone number. Then print your own.

- Instead of purchasing several expensive accounting books, invest in one pack of hole-punched analysis paper and some cheap cardboard binders. No waste, no large initial outlay.

- You can't afford a purpose-built office? A desk tucked into a recess somewhere in your home, with shelves for storage up to the ceiling, will be adequate for a start. (My first desk was no more than a piece of timber mounted inside a doorless cupboard.)

- You can't afford a secretary but you can't type! Either learn, or advertise for a homeworker who would be flexible and paid only by the hour.

There are certain other items it is unwise to economise on. Your business cards and letterheadings will be your first contact with your potential new clients and should be nicely typeset and printed. However, embossed two-colour efforts are unnecessary. If you decide on single colour printing, black on white paper looks most prestigious.

10

NEW VENTURES

It is advisable of course to launch into business with some knowledge of your product or service and to research the market before taking action. You may, however, find new ideas that interest you along the way and consider adding another string to your bow. The danger in this is that in becoming too absorbed in a new project you may not give sufficient attention to your original enterprise. Ideally:

- The new idea should fit in well with your existing business.

- You have engaged staff who are sufficiently trustworthy to stand in for you while you are exploring new avenues.

Otherwise, should the new idea fail, you may be faced with the daunting prospect of picking up the pieces and trying to put your business together again.

How a Change of Direction May Occur

I started as a print farmer, having had a little experience as a printer's representative. A print farmer is someone who calls on companies with a view to supplying their printing needs – forms, headings, leaflets and nowadays printed computer stationery. He or she then 'farms' it out to the printers whose equipment is most suited economically for the work. In other words, the farmer acts as a broker or agent.

Most companies do not care for print farmers, preferring to deal direct, but obviously one does not advertise the fact that one does not actually own the works and equipment.

Unfortunately printers too resent farmers. This is reflected in a derisive term they use for describing them – 'Armchair Printers'. The reality of the situation may be quite different, but there is a wide gap of misunderstanding between Production and Sales, even internally within companies.

But as a businessman a printer will not turn away good work and understands the necessity for good prices to allow for the farmer's mark-up.

After I had been farming print for about a year, one of my clients asked me for some stationery items. To buy time I bought these items from Ryman's, supplied my client and then set about contacting stationery wholesalers. One thing led to another and I became a 'Brass-Plate Stationer'. This is another derogatory term, which applies to a person who sells stationery and office supplies but has no stock.

My first stationery wholesale contact produced a catalogue with a blank cover for use by dealers. I bought a number of copies, stapled a business card to each front cover and distributed them to my print clients. Orders to my wholesaler were initially in the smallest acceptable quantities to fill my clients' needs and I had to work hard, collecting the goods, packing them and delivering them to my clients more quickly and efficiently than my competitors.

Now I have exchanged my 'Brass Plate' for valuable stocks, and office supplies are the mainstay of my business. Printing I still handle, but see it as an extra if it comes along with the stationery. I do not promote it, since I have no practical experience of running a machine works and cannot see my future in developing that side of the business.

The control I have over my office supplies business and the asset value of my stock is more rewarding.

11

TIMING

Timing is often a critical factor in business. One of the most trying aspects of timing is deciding when to cut your losses, i.e. being *able* to settle upon that turning point when efforts have been made to give a project a fair chance and yet it seems it would be foolhardy to continue.

At one time I rented a shop, thinking it would be a useful sideline to my commercial stationery business. For many reasons it proved both time-consuming and unprofitable. My normal commercial turnover dropped dramatically and I experienced a bad financial patch.

I cut my losses, relinquished the shop and returned to my former method of trading. Immediately my turnover rocketed and in 4 months I was solvent again.

Yet another situation occurred where I could easily have thrown in the towel and subsequently lost a potentially valuable client. I had spent some time wooing this client with little success. As his company was large, with a high stationery consumption, I continued to call long after one would normally have given up. My patience paid off. The business dealings began in earnest for me after the buyer I was calling on left the company.

Ironically, although he gave me precious little business, he was so impressed by my set-up (at the time I was running a 1-ton Volkswagen van kitted out with shelves like a miniature supermarket) that he decided to implement an identical enterprise himself. During the time I had been calling on him I had cultivated friendly terms with the other staff, and fortunately for me his successor was a person to whom I related very well.

After my original contact had done his best to pick my brain about contacts and procedures, he tried to persuade his former employers to use his services, but I was fortunate. They kept their business with me.

When to abort? There can be no hard and fast rule for good timing, as the above anecdotes demonstrate. Intuition is as reliable a method as any I know.

Everyone at times makes wrong decisions, but it is a waste of time and totally destructive to grieve about what is past and unchangeable.

12

ANALYSIS

Analyse your business personality by doing this quiz. Be truthful. A successful businesswoman must always be totally honest with herself.

1 Your work is unfairly criticised by a client who is normally reasonable in his dealings with you. Do you:

  (a) Wonder if he may be right? Perhaps you should have checked with your senior before acting.

  (b) Think, 'Oh well, never mind, perhaps he's had a bad day' and deal with his complaint as calmly as possible, without compromising yourself?

  (c) Get defensive and rather upset?

  (d) Send him a bill for your work and ask your secretary to say you're out when next he calls?

2 You receive a visit from an unknown but persistent caller. Do you:

  (a) Tell him you're so sorry, but he'll have to excuse you because you have another engagement? Then sit chewing your nails in frustration because he won't go.

  (b) Tell him you don't see anyone without a prior

appointment and to write to you explaining the nature of his call? Ask your secretary to show him out?

(c) Hide quickly in the stationery cupboard and tell your secretary to say you've gone home?

(d) Tell him in no uncertain terms where to go?

3 You are lunching a client and accidentally knock over the wine. To your horror, it deposits its contents right into his lap. Do you:

(a) Cover your face in humiliation and shrink into your chair?

(b) Quickly pass him every available napkin within your reach and ensure there is a treble whisky awaiting him on his return from the gents?

(c) Flap and make a great fuss, drawing everyone's attention to your joint embarrassment?

(d) Say, 'Don't worry. I'll order another bottle?'

4 You lost a sum of money due to your own (uncharacteristic) negligence. Do you:

(a) Feel distraught and angry with yourself and find it impossible to concentrate on your work?

(b) Feel peeved, but try to take it philosophically? It must happen to everyone sometime. You will be more careful in the future.

(c) Tearfully telephone the man in your life and pour out your heart? After all, that's what lovers are for.

(d) Find a good reason to justify yourself and feel annoyed that life is so unfair?

5 You secretary asks for 3 days off the week you are away

on business. She is most persuasive but the situation would be desperately inconvenient for you. Do you:

(a) Cancel your business trip?

(b) Insist that you need her services that week? Your trip could be very good for the firm and if your deal came off, it could well be instrumental in a rise for her.

(c) Argue with her as to whose trip was more important?

(d) Refuse without giving good reason?

6 You have made a promise which, due to circumstances outside your control, you cannot honour. Do you:

(a) Ignore the problem, hoping fervently that it will go away?

(b) Telephone your contact immediately, explain briefly and apologise?

(c) Worry about it all day, then force yourself to telephone at 4.58, hoping that your contact has already left to catch his train?

(d) Get your secretary to write a letter? You've got more important things to think about.

7 You are treated rudely by a colleague's new secretary. Do you:

(a) Try to make yourself inconspicuous behind the office cheeseplant?

(b) Think of a sharp put-down, put her down and forget it?

(c) Report her angrily to your colleague?

(d) Say, 'Do you *know* who *I* am?'

8 Your client demands a delivery date which you know you cannot adhere to. Do you:

(a) Feel awkward about refusing and go all around the houses in your attempts to do so?

(b) Tell him straight! You would like this job very much, but you would prefer to decline than make a rash promise and then let him down.

(c) Apologise to him profusely for being unable to help him in this instance and then give him ten excuses for your failure to co-operate?

(d) Tell him you will do it and hope it will be all right on the night? After all, your competitors would probably do the same.

9 You answer the telephone yourself because your secretary has left early. 'Mr Perkins, please,' says a new, potential client. 'I'm Jane Perkins,' you reply. 'I want to speak to the boss,' he barks officiously, '*Mr* Perkins. Who would that be, your husband, your father . . .?' How do you respond?

(a) Apologetically? 'Actually there's no Mr Perkins. I'm Miss Perkins. Could I help you?'

(b) Matter-of-factly? 'I am Jane Perkins and I am the owner of Perkins Marketing. Can I help you?'

(c) Indignantly? 'You're *speaking* to the boss of Perkins Marketing.'

(d) Aggressively? 'My old man left me 6 months ago and my dad drives a dustcart. I think you'd better talk to me as I'm the only Perkins available in this outfit.'

10 You decide to run a franchise business with your husband. He receives a letter from Head Office,

requesting him to go along to sign a contract. There is a postscript to the letter. It suggests he brings along his wife as there is to be a little talk afterwards about future promotional prospects. Do you:

(a) Have a little moan to your old man, but otherwise do the right thing and trot along by his side exactly as is expected of you?

(b) Put on your sharpest business suit and ensure that the agenda also includes a little talk by you about the principles of partnership?

(c) Get very irate and refuse to go to the meeting?

(d) Go to the meeting, but when you get there, make some outrageous symbolic gesture, like setting fire to the contract or grossly insulting the Head Chauvinist?

Now check your rating.

Mostly A Ratings

Well, maybe your lack of confidence is due to conditioning. Nevertheless it would need to be overcome before you could seriously contemplate improving your status in business. In fact, if you scored entirely As, there is a good chance that you and your secretary would soon be swapping places.

However, if you scored half As and the remainder of your score consisted of Bs, there is hope for you. Stop apologising and remember you are entitled to your point of view. What you believe is an essential part of you, your ego, your personality and your sense of self-respect.

Study the B answers where you scored As, then get out into the big, wide world and practise asserting yourself.

Mostly B Ratings

If your score was entirely composed of Bs, all I can say is, 'Hi, Businesswoman of the Year!' You can hardly fail. You have just the right balance of positive reaction and assertiveness, yet with no hint of being dogmatic. Seldom will you lose your cool head, whatever the emergency.

If you scored mostly Bs accompanied by a high proportion of Ds, you could queer your pitch occasionally by being too hard-headed. Business means getting on with people, unless you have some particular talent which sets you apart from the crowd. Try to show a little more sympathy.

If the rest of your score was predominantly As or Cs, you need to build up your sense of confidence and calm. Study the B answers to your A and C responses.

Mostly C Ratings

A score of more than five Cs indicates that you are far too emotional to be happy in business. You react instinctively and relate to the responses of others in a personal and defensive way. No doubt you have skills in other directions, maybe creative or artistic leanings. There is nothing wrong with this, if it is what suits you best, but your passionate and impetuous nature would certainly be crushed by the realities and injustices of business life.

However, if you scored five C's, four Bs and maybe one A, you may stand a chance, but accept that you have a long way to go. Your success would entirely depend upon your determination in learning to keep your cool.

Mostly D Ratings

You tend to be inflexible at times, don't you! You are tough enough to handle the rigours of business life, but you will turn away opportunities by your stubbornness and hard-headedness. That is not to say you may not be right in your evaluations, but remember that discretion is the better part of valour and that empathy can partner toughness without demeaning its effectiveness.

If your D answers are fairly balanced with Bs, I think that by cultivating self-discipline you might operate very well.

Anyone with a majority of Ds is, I believe, unlikely to have scored a balance in As and/or Cs. If you have, then I suspect you have not answered the quiz truthfully.

Check it out again more carefully.

SEXUAL HARASSMENT

Although it is accepted that female employees can be, and are, subject to sexual harassment in spite of the fact that there are now laws to try to protect them, it seems to be a common misconception that if you are running your own show, or have progressed to senior status in your field, you do not suffer from this kind of victimisation. That is not so.

A senior businesswoman may, for reasons of status, respect and the law, be inviolate within her own company, yet encounter difficulty when negotiating with executives from the company's associates and clients. It could be that the goodwill of these people is instrumental in her maintaining her position and credibility, and their business of value to her firm.

If you are a woman going it alone, you may not stand to lose everything because one or two business contacts persist in pushing their luck, but it can be a headache if you are used to their business. There is no one senior to whom you can appeal for help. The law can't help you. Even if it tried, it couldn't stop the contact from withdrawing its business.

Before proceeding further, I would like to define what I see as sexual harassment. Obviously some man will try it on, but after he has been politely rebuffed, what then? If he continues to plague you with unwanted attention, sexual innuendos, leery invitations to dinner and 'afters', lecherous smirks and snide remarks about 'all the business you're getting', then I reckon that's sexual harassment.

[75]

You can say that you're already attached, but regrettably that does not always work.

Once a company I was dealing with (it was my second largest account) took on a new chap on a retainer basis and he was placed in charge of purchasing my products. I won't go into details, but he gave me a bad time. My secretary and I spent fruitless hours trying to figure out how best I should handle him. Nothing seemed to work to dampen his ardour. Yet the account was one of our most profitable and had been since long before he came on to the scene.

It seemed somehow unprofessional to report him to his MD. If I had taken this course, and they were happy with his work, I am sure I would have been the one to drown in the waves that I was making.

I had almost decided to stop calling on him, when he was unceremoniously thrown out. It appeared he had been abusing his business expense account on what were ostensibly business lunches but had more to do with young women 'prospects' of a different kind.

This was a very difficult situation and my first experience of this particularly contemptuous form of sexual blackmail, but I think it taught me a few techniques for keeping such unpleasant characters at bay. Therefore I would say, do adopt, if possible, the same principles towards your SOB (Sexually Overactive Buyer) as you would towards your taxman. Don't rely on evasion, that is asking for trouble. Do, however, AVOID.

Evasive Techniques – The Wrong Way

Apart from the fact that using one-off evasive excuses indicates that you have already allowed an unacceptable degree of familiarity to enter into the relationship, such excuses only solve the problem of the moment, e.g.

You: But we only met last week.

SOB: (thinks) If I play my cards right, I should score *next* week, especially if I get her tipsy.

You: It's the wrong time of the month.

SOB: (thinks) Should be all right by Tuesday.

You: I couldn't possibly. I'm not like that/interested in sex/in love with you/a two-man woman.

SOB: (thinks) Oh boy, I could really get my teeth into this one!

Avoidance Techniques – the Right Way

The best way of avoiding sexual harassment is to maintain a barrier by keeping your dealings with any new business associates on a formal footing, at least until you have assured yourself that your contact is a man of integrity. Avoiding the use of his Christian name, overtly sexy clothes, and that extra glass of wine when you lunch him, will assist in maintaining the equilibrium.

If, in despite of these precautions, you still experience difficulty, consider the following:

(a) Are there certain times of the day when your SOB is less likely to be alone, or has a daily chore to perform in the company of others? Remember there is safety in numbers. If he has to discuss raw material availability each day with Jones from Production at precisely 11 am, call on him at 10.50.

(b) Don't ever put yourself in jeopardy. For instance, never call on him 15 minutes before lunch or office closing time (unless, of course, his girl friend from Accounts regularly searches him out at these times).

(c) If you're brave, you could think of a good reason why you should call him urgently at home on a business matter. Whether the call is received by him or his wife, do be matter of fact about it (she may be listening on the bedroom extension and the poor woman probably has enough to put up with already).

Although your call must appear to be entirely above board, it could put the fear of God into your SOB and solve your problem without losing you his business.

(d) Threaten him *subtly* with a very jealous and extremely large lover. Don't say your lover is a black belt in judo. It's not original and won't work. Mention casually in passing (and not just when he has been particularly obnoxious, as that will seem contrived) how your lover once made a nasty mess of a man in a pub who kept looking at you. Make a vague reference to Intensive Care as if it slightly embarrasses you, and if he looks suitably impressed by your story, mutter something about a writ for GBH, just for good measure. If your lover is particularly large and macho, or if you have a friend who fits the bill and does not object to acting out a role for the sake of your peace of mind and your progress, do try to find out where your SOB drinks and arrange a 'chance' meeting.

It is much better of course not to get to the stage where one has to take such drastic measures, and I would like to emphasise the point that by conforming to old-fashioned standards of behaviour, quite an effective barrier can be maintained in most cases. Whether this cooling effect arises from an increased respect for one's womanhood, or whether it is total confusion as to what makes one tick, is neither here nor there.

However, if everything fails and you cannot stand it any

more, and you decide his business or his support just isn't worth the hassle, you might as well go down fighting. Try the best put-down I ever used against an accusation of frigidity.

'Not at all. It's just that *you* don't inspire me!'

INTERDEPARTMENTAL CONFLICT

Although it may be some time before you have to deal with this within your own set-up, it is useful to understand something of the system while you are working your way up, so that by the time you are head of your department, or running your own show, you will be fully experienced and able to deal with the back-biting rife between departments. Even better, you may be able to rise entirely above it.

Even if you decide to go on the road and sell, a knowledge of the war between the departments will help you to deal with your clients with skill and diplomacy. Let us consider a typical medium-sized manufacturing company.

Production

The worst enemy of Production is Sales. Production considers that Sales has a jolly easy time of it, socialising, taking clients to lunch, enjoying bottomless expense accounts which are used on plush hotels and early evening drinks with buddies. Actually Production is rather jealous of Sales.

Production grumbles incessantly about its overloaded schedules, its lack of tea breaks and how it is not appreciated. Production has either not enough overtime or too much overtime.

Production goes on strike for many different reasons incomprehensible to other departments. It could be over a punch-up among staff, it could be because one of the packers was asked to run a machine, it could be because a non-union worker was taken on, even though there was no union man available with his specialised qualifications.

A factory worker must never be asked to help a supplier's delivery driver to unload a consignment of raw material. If there is no one else available to do it, the van has to depart with its load still intact.

Production spends a great deal of time having meetings during working hours, but always clocks out at 5.00 p.m. sharp. Unless of course it is getting paid double time for staying later.

Sales

Sales sees itself as a scapegoat and a troubleshooter. But mostly as a scapegoat.

When Production commits a blunder, Sales always takes the rap. Sales works itself to death, operating under all kinds of pressures, only to be let down again by Production on delivery dates and quality.

Sales has to make an effort to get along with Production, because, after all, Production has the upper hand. If Production isn't treated with kid gloves, it might have a tantrum and go on strike, just when there is a vital delivery date to adhere to, thereby endangering Sales' critical turnover figures and even more critical salespeople's commissions. Sales also gets angry with Estimating for taking 3 weeks to produce a quotation and for being 30 per cent over the top.

Most of all Sales hates Credit Control for clipping its wings when soliciting new business. Credit Control takes far too long approving references, thereby losing precious orders from new prospects, and frequently cuts off Sales' No. 1

Customer's supplies because he exceeded his settlement limit by 2 days.

Sales complains a great deal about having to lunch with customers it cannot stand. Nonetheless, it takes 3 hours doing so and goes home afterwards totally exhausted.

Credit Control

Being steeped in secrecy and surrounded by systems and printouts that nobody else understands, Credit Control enjoys a certain mystique which other departments do not enjoy. Naturally, as it takes care of the payments, Credit Control considers itself the heart and life-blood of the company.

Credit Control's main quarrel is with Sales's Area Managers. In its opinion they are too obsessed with targets and do not impress upon their salespeople the necessity for thoroughly interrogating and investigating new clients for creditworthiness, and for taking orders before references have been received and approved.

Bought Ledger

Bought Ledger's main beef is with Purchasing, which seems to spend its time harassing it to pay suppliers in accordance with the latter's terms and conditions. Bought Ledger tends to think it is a law unto itself and that suppliers are jolly fortunate to be paid at all.

Personnel

In its own area Personnel enjoys God-like stature. The decision to say yes or no, to approve or disapprove, lies in Personnel's power. Personnel has been responsible for giving birth to the Company Family, and each staff member, as a hopeful new applicant, has chewed his or her fingernails outside Personnel's interview room. (Excepting of course the MD's son, the Chairman's brother and the Secretary and Treasurer's mistress.)

If Personnel occasionally gets too big for its boots, that may be understandable. But this is apt to make it unpopular with other departments, to which it has assigned the occasional misfit.

Purchasing

Providing it is an efficient unit, Purchasing probably relates quite well to other departments, except Bought Ledger, whose laxness in paying the bills causes Purchasing a constant headache with suppliers, who are reluctant to continue supplying without being paid. Bought Ledger is never at fault. The delay is either due to the second signatory being away on business, postal delays or a batch of missing invoices. This is not much help to Purchasing, which has Production on its heels because the factory has come to a standstill due to a lack of polystyrene bubbles to pack the goods in.

Apart from this, Purchasing jogs along day by day in reasonable harmony with the rest of the departments, *if* at great personal cost. (It isn't easy getting all those last-minute deliveries organised, and most Purchasing Managers have bitten-down fingernails.)

But at least when Purchasing has a really bad day, it has ample opportunity to give release to its stress by unleashing its venom on visiting sales people.

15

WOMEN AND THE PROFESSIONAL SERVICES

Banks

A woman client of mine is so in awe of her bank manager, who treats her with thinly disguised contempt, that she takes her accountant with her for moral support whenever she has a meeting with him. If you find yourself saddled with a bank that is unhelpful, inefficient or even over-cautious, move your account elsewhere.

I cannot emphasise enough that to find a bank with an approach that is both realistic and sympathetic is important to anyone in business. There can be tremendous differences in attitudes even between branches of the same High Street banking chain.

How to deal with your bank manager

If your personal bank account is in credit most of the time, you might be wise to stick with that bank. If it is permanently in the red and you've bounced a few cheques, it would be preferable to put your business account elsewhere. But don't expect a massive overdraft until you have been able to show a healthy, fast-moving account.

Don't meet your bank manager looking destitute. If you have some good jewellery, wear it. If not, borrow a few large rocks and a heavy gold charm bracelet from your well heeled friend.

If you smoke, don't roll your own.

Take a notebook in which you have carefully logged all the points you wish to make, research you have done, contacts you have made and how you intend to survive and make your business pay. During the interview refer to your notebook at frequent intervals, and whenever your bank manager mentions something that seems to be important, nod your head thoughtfully and write it down.

If this does not work, try another branch or even another bank.

Despite their traditional image, however, banks *are* changing. They are in a competitive business too and are there to give you a service, not to grant audiences. Don't be surprised if you are interviewed by a woman bank manager, as many female assistant branch managers are on their way up.

That is exactly what banks need to help them change faster!

Accountants

Accountants are a necessary evil.

At best, an Accountant is a barrier between you and the lurking bogeymen that prey on the natural weaknesses of hardworking business people. I mean of course the Inland Revenue and the gentlemen at HM Customs and Excise.

The Accountant is there to avert disaster, though one that may by default have been instigated by him in the first place.

I have employed several accountants in my time, so have experienced varying degrees of ineptitude. I have escaped fines and court appearances by the skin of my teeth, as such mundane items as balance sheets and deduction cards have been reluctantly submitted by my current accountant the day before it seems I was to be dragged, kicking and screaming, to account for my tardiness.

At the end of the day, however, it's always down to the poor, harassed business person. Yet accountants seem to know just how far they can go before provoking the said bogeymen into action, and only once have I actually been bitten.

My first accountant, on seeing my humble beginnings in a hard and competitive world, assumed my business would fold up after the first year of trading. To my horror I discovered my company had been de-registered. When I tackled him about the notice, he merely shrugged and remarked, 'I didn't think you could carry on'.

So don't look to your accountant for a source of inspiration. Accountants deal in facts, not fantasies. It is the entrepreneur who turns fantasy into reality.

How to Deal with Your Accountant

First, get the right one if you can. Remember, you need someone who is more than merely a mechanic with figures. Ask the proprietor of a small business whom you know quite well for a recommendation. Some accountants are more in tune with small businesses than others, and it is better for you if the one you choose is really interested in handling your work.

Don't try to pull the wool over your accountant's eyes; it is not in your interests to do so. An accountant is to your finances as a doctor is to the health of your body. Make it clear you mean business. State a date by which you must have all your books and documents returned to you. It doesn't mean you'll get them. But it does show you mean business and I'm sure that helps.

Unless you have plenty of cash to splash around, make the effort to visit your accountant's offices, as 'house calls' are likely to increase the final bill.

Have a notebook handy with all relevant points to ensure you do not waste any time. Chatting about irrelevancies could cost you £30.00 per hour. If you can supply the essential data, your accountant will set a clerk to do the groundwork and use his or her own skills to determine the most advantageous representation of your business to the relevant authorities and to advise you upon your future strategy.

If you are not satisfied, never be afraid to make a change. Remember, you are the client and you are the one who is paying!

16

OVERCOMING OBSTACLES

A telephone and an answering machine are so-called 'essentials' when starting out as a self-employed or business person, yet I managed without either of these devices for the first few months. The birth of my business coincided with a house move, my new flat was phone-less and the waiting list prohibitive. I persuaded a friend who was also in business to take messages so that I could later contact my potential clients from a callbox. This is not recommended.

No Telephone?

After you have managed to locate a callbox that is both empty and unvandalised and begun dialling frantically, a pile of 10p coins at the ready on the directory shelf, you may suddenly spot the queue of angry people impatiently shuffling their feet and stamping about in the rain outside your box. This is both embarrassing and off-putting. You may feel obliged to conclude your call and join the end of the queue.

No Answerphone?

Messages *do* slip the net.

Of course the above instances are rather extreme situations. When you bite off more than you can chew, inevitably you suffer for it. Just the same, I think it is worth considering how trivial impediments are if you have real ambition. Whatever the complication, there is almost always a way around it if you mean business and are determined to win.

Marilyn Hunter, Hunters Chartered Accountants

Marilyn, who runs her own highly successful accountancy business, is a true professional who always retains the personal touch. Her status in life has come about through a combination of several quirks of fate, a few major catastrophes and, of course, her own determined will to find something better – and win!

(Having met and talked in depth to Marilyn, I confess that had I met her *before* I wrote my piece on accountants, my view might have been less rigid!)

Marilyn gained nine O-Levels after an ordinary grammar school education and decided to become a pathologist. She went for some interviews, was shown around the hospital laboratories but had a sneaking suspicion there was something better to do than potter amongst the pickled jars.

At the time, her brother worked for a firm of accountants, and her parents, who were always supportive, suggested that she have a word with her brother's boss. That talk gave her a great deal to think about. She decided that she liked the idea of working within her own self-applied parameters.

Her first job in accountancy was with a small, friendly firm that demanded little in the area of qualifications and gave her autonomy in looking after certain clients. Marilyn readily admits that this cosy situation made her rather complacent, for having got only halfway through her examinations she did not proceed to her finals.

But then her firm folded up and she was made redundant.

[90]

'I was out of work on my wedding day. It was terrible!' she tells me.

She decided to find a job with a larger company, hoping it would give her more security.

'In the begining I shared a room with other senior people, because the company was expanding. But suddenly I was moved out and given a jumble-sale desk. I can only assume that a complaint was made against me because I did not have my qualifications.'

Marilyn, in turn, was not impressed by the company.

'The larger company's hierarchy made clients pay for every level of work. First there would be the articled clerk, then the senior manager and eventually, when a situation came to a head, the partner. The chances were that the partner would not know anything about the case and by this time, the client would have clocked up so many hours on each level, that the bill would be astronomical.

'I did my share of "ticking and hoping". That's an inside term for the many hours spent by clerks going through endless columns of ledgers, ticking off and hoping that eventually they would reach the end. There was no variety. You never saw a job through to the client. It was more like a factory assembly line.'

She stuck it for just six weeks.

Marilyn says that the pleasure in accountancy comes from participating, not just adding up all the time. She feels that an accountant must be a member of a team, with the client on top, the accountant on one side and the bank manager on the other.

If the trio clicks, it should result in successful business.

Marilyn got her first chances through friends starting up in business, who asked her to do their books for them. She did this in her own time, in conjunction with a regular job. Her husband, who was also self-employed, introduced her to some of his own contacts and other businesspeople found her service through the Yellow Pages. She found that many of these new clients had become sick to death of dealing with the larger firms with the same dual combination of high fees and poor service.

Then the Institute of Chartered Accountants brought out a restriction setting a time limit for completing examinations to qualify as a Chartered Accountant. It was just the push that Marilyn needed. She got her skates on and did her finals.

'I qualified in 1980,' says Marilyn, 'and from that moment, the doors opened up for me.'

But there was still one obstacle to overcome. Once qualified, a new Chartered Accountant is expected to serve a training apprenticeship and is not permitted to practise immediately. Marilyn appealed against this rule, putting forward her experience and reinforcing her argument with letters of recommendation from her previous employers, which convinced the Institute that she would make a competent, practising accountant. Her practising certificate was granted.

So Marilyn took the tremendous step of relinquishing her job to become a full-time self-employed Chartered Accountant.

'You wonder how long it will take to fill the void, but it worked out for me. My previous employer wished me luck and wanted to retain my services on a sub-contract basis. I also acquired several new clients through recommendation. This tided me over the period that had worried me.'

In 1983, Marilyn's husband had to give up his business through ill-health and subsequently became involved in Marilyn's company.

'In the beginning, you could sense there was a deep feeling of unhappiness in him. He had been accustomed to being the major breadwinner. At this difficult time, I felt it was important to communicate, to talk about the problems, to voice our thoughts. I tried to *involve* him. We overcame this potentially explosive situation and he became a conscientious and productive member of my team. He did not mind what he did for me. I think the transition was made easier because, having been self-employed himself, he understood the complexities of accountancy.

I asked Marilyn if she had experienced any difficulties in succeeding in business as a woman. She said she had not had any major problems, since being fully qualified. To a degree she felt her professional status protected her from discrimination. (I suspect it might also have something to do with an aura of brisk efficiency which somehow manages never to be off-putting.)

'There was *one* occasion recently when I was rather cross, I was going to an extremely important meeting with one of my major clients, and an associate told me to "put on my best frock." Well, *really!'*

Marilyn now owns a beautiful property in the Green Belt worth over a quarter million, complete with ducks, geese and visiting red-legged partridges. Her recipe for success?

'Never lose sight of the fact that the client is *important.* Never forget that the client is entitled to a reasonable standard of work *at all times.'*

Maureen Sampson

Obviously not all obstacles faced by women in business are directly related to their sex. But one does hear some pretty appalling stories from women who have succeeded despite gross mistreatment.

Maureen worked for 10 years as a book-keeper for a proprietor of a shopfitting/French polishing business. Eventually he made her company secretary. The firm did well. When he decided to sell the business, Maureen offered to buy it. 'Don't be so silly', he said.

The company was sold to a man of 30 who just could not cope, who had no experience and who wouldn't listen to anyone. In 21 weeks he spent all the money and ran it into the ground. People who had worked for the company for 35 years found themselves without a job.

In an effort to save the company one of the male staff

decided to go after a loan, but he was interested only in the joinery side. Maureen, however, knew all about the other side of the business – French polishing.

'My colleague was around 55, lived in a rented flat and had no regard for his appearance. He did not bother to prepare anything for the bank to prove his worthiness.

'I decided to go after a loan too, so that I could pursue my own interest, the French polishing. I spent 3 months carefully formulating my case, my whole *curriculum vitae*, my business ideas, my cash-flow forecast. I was prepared to put my house on the line. Together we went to the bank with our accountant.

'My colleague was in the bank for just fifteen minutes – he came out beaming.

'The bank manager's office was pretty intimidating, desk almost as big as a room, great marble pillars. The bank manager didn't help. He sat there and stared at me . . . and stared and stared . . .

'He did not speak to me once, only to my accountant.

'"Why have you brought a woman to see me?" he said. "Total rubbish. It could never work."

'Then he spoke to me. "You should be home, looking after your children."'

Maureen pointed out that her children were quite old enough to look after themselves. 'Maybe your husband might want to have more children,' snarled the bank manager.

'I just couldn't believe it,' says Maureen. 'I had spent 3 months of my life putting together that proposition and all he wanted to discuss was my reproductive organs.'

To be fair, legislation now protects women from this sort of treatment, and, as we all know, banks are making conscious efforts to update their image and be more sympathetic towards small businesses and women in business. Nevertheless all this happened only 5 years ago!

It is to Maureen's credit that she overcame this apparently immovable obstacle by simply walking around it. She managed without the loan. She started up her business in disused farm buildings, restoring antique furniture. She expanded, moved to new premises and ventured into joinery, specialising in pine furniture and kitchens.

She is now looking for new, larger premises and employs fourteen people. As for her old colleague, the one who got his loan sorted out in 15 minutes, he went bankrupt after 9 months!

Unfortunately for Maureen, however, the emotional scars run deep. 'I'm good at what I do,' she said, 'and I know I could make a fortune, but I can't bring myself to go to the bank and ask them for a loan.'

She did, however, seem a little happier when I told her about that new phenomenon – the woman bank manager!

17

MARKETING

Marketing is a subject everyone professes to know a bit about yet few people are able to define. I asked a cross-section of men and women to explain to me their personal concept of marketing.

- It's packaging and all that stuff. It's making the counter display look attractive.

- It's not advertising hearing aids in teenage magazines or trying to sell cola near an old people's home.

- It's like when a firm promotes a new brand of shampoo and wants to find out the best colour fluid and shape of bottle to appeal to the consumer.

- It's girls with big boobs lying all over Porsches at motor shows (this one from a man of course!).

- It's the walnut on top of a walnut whip (I loved this one!).

In order to get an expert's definition I asked Rob Carter, ex-lecturer in both selling and marketing.

'Selling and marketing are two entirely different areas,' he told me. 'Marketing is the art of drawing together the buyer and the seller, up to the point of sale. After that it's up to the salesperson to make or break the deal.'

Rob has worked with both men and women in marketing and talks highly of the women's performance. Women have, it seems, a natural aptitude in this highly creative and deeply psychological field.

So marketing is about making your product or service attractive so that it achieves the maximum response. It's about getting it to the right market at the right time.

It is about advertising, from press advertising to the more personal mailshot. It is about promotion, using introductory offers or free gifts (like the plastic toy inside a box of corn-flakes). It is about the 'free to enter' competition, if you answer one simple question and make up a slogan. (It isn't really free because you've got to send in five chocolate bar wrappers with your entry form.)

The Department of Trade recently stated that of 1.4 million businesses in the United Kingdom, 1.35 million are smaller firms. Yet there is no reason why these smaller firms, even those on a tight budget, cannot copy the techniques used by the large organisations.

There are many ways in which small companies can benefit from established marketing principles.

A large company might spend millions getting its pack-aging right – the design, the colour. Imagine therefore that you have started up your own estate agency. Like the pack-aging in the supermarket, your 'For Sale' board needs to be colourful and eyecatching. It stands to reason that a bright primary colour like yellow or red as a predominant feature will be more successful than a subdued shade of blue or grey.

Says Maggie Sheridan of her small but very upmarket bou-tique, 'I have the window changed weekly – it *is* the point of sale. I try to make it topical by introducing a theme, like Ascot or Henley.'

At the moment the window has a golfing theme, with clubs and balls artfully worked into the display.

Maggie says, 'This week we're sponsoring pro-am' (profes-sional and amateur golfing event) 'and for every amateur who gets a "hole in one" there will be a prize of £100.00.'

Large outfits can afford to have their names splashed around town in neon lights. But a businesswoman friend of mine has done proportionately well with a cheery poster that travels around on the backs of London buses.

So how can you apply marketing to your own situation?

You Can't Afford a Television Commercial?

Contact your local cinema. For many standard types of businesses there are ready-made commercials on to which your name and sound-recording can be imposed, so you don't even need to find the cash to shoot your own film. If you are small, your preferred area of operation is probably local, so what more do you need?

You Can't Afford Press Advertising?

Are you sure? Maybe the national dailies are out, but how about supporting your local rag? You can have a larger, more imposing spread for far less outlay than in the national press. But first identify your market. If you are in engineering, a trade journal advertisement might be more advantageous.

Mailshots

Mailshots are another method which can be as ostentatious and expensive or as cheap and cheerful as you can afford. If your budget allows it, you could have a beautiful, glossy colour brochure printed, and there are agencies who will handle the design, the printing and the distribution. On the other hand, you could simply type up your blurb, get it duplicated or photocopied and mail it out yourself to put it through likely doors. Perhaps for some pocket money you could hire a couple of youngsters to do the footwork for you.

If you do decide to do a mailshot, bear in mind that the normal return is only 1 per cent. This might seem low, but it may be worthwhile as a means of getting your name known, particularly if the 1 per cent you realise is 'repeat' business. Your mailshot must have impact, so if you cannot afford to hire artistic help, ensure your copy is well presented, with clear, bright objectives.

It is a good idea to follow up your mailshot with another. In direct mailing persistence pays off.

Mailing lists can be bought from mailing houses. Or maybe you could compile your own through Yellow Pages or the *Business Classified Directory*.

To summarise:

(a) *Do Your Homework First*. I can best demonstrate this by recounting an alarming story. A company that had spent in excess of £100,000 on press advertising for its new slim French biscuit, was suddenly caught short. Having gone through all the paraphernalia of market research, advertising, and careful packaging, they had to withdraw all their biscuits because the Weights and Measures people discovered the incorrect weight had been printed on the packet. Millions of self-adhesive labels had to be printed in a hurry to correct the error.

(b) *Make a Budget Allowance*. Lots of small companies resent spending money on advertising, but this can be a false economy in the long run. As I have shown, you can 'cut your cloth' to suit. Setting aside an annual budget for advertising could well increase your business turnover accordingly.

(c) *Identify Your Market*. What sort of market are you seeking? Young, old, trendy, traditional? Is your method going to *reach* that market? Is it slanted so that it will appeal to that

[99]

market? Is it image-conscious? A little subtle flattery can be beguiling.

Identify your market – then go for it!

18

PATRONISING PEOPLE

I think it is fair to say that one's status and self-image feed off each other, i.e. the higher your self-esteem, the easier to achieve status. The more that you feel you are achieving status, the more confident you will become. But you will still have to allow for Other People.

There will be occasions, both social and business, when you will be subtly insulted. This is not made any easier by the fact that the other party is probably blissfully unaware that he or she is trivialising your accomplishments:

Middle-aged upper class lady at a social gathering: 'Hello, so you're Janet. Do tell me, what's it like being a business tycoon?'
Me: 'I really don't know. Do you?'

Newly employed but inconsiderate son: 'Mum, can you take my suit to the cleaners?'
Me: 'What do you think I am. Take it yourself.'
Son: 'But I'm *working*!'

Proprietor of the studio that took my bookjacket photo: 'What's your book about?'
Me: 'It's about being a woman in business.'
Prop.: 'Oh, you mean cream teas, that sort of thing?'

(I am not for one moment suggesting that running a success-ful business serving cream teas is any less valid than any other enterprise, but why do men assume that women can only handle traditionally female areas? It's about as logical as women expecting all men to be plumbers.)

Here is an encounter with a salesman at a stall in a Business Exhibition which I attended with a male associate:

Salesman: 'Can I help you, Madam?'
Me: Yes, please. I'm interested in your range. Could you give me some more information, literature, prices that sort of thing?
Salesman: 'Certainly, just a moment.'
(Meanwhile my business associate wanders over and joins us.)
Salesman: 'Right, sir, here are the leaflets your secretary asked for and you might be interested to know we can also provide . . .'
Me: . . . . . . ! ! ! ! ! !

The Managing Director of a supplier and I, while discussing the technicalities of a £7,000 print job I had placed with him, had the following exhange:

MD: 'Well, I think that just about wraps it up.'
Me: Yes, I can't think of anything else.
MD: 'Well, I can't stand around here discussing one job when I have £50,000 worth of work to deal with in the machine room.'

. . . and I was a CUSTOMER ! ! ! ! ! !
People being patronising, people being thoughtless, or just sour grapes from me? But could any of these incidents have happened to a man?

19

DELEGATION

The way in which you handle delegation within the confines of your own set-up is a personal thing. It may depend to a degree on the size and type of business, your own personal leadership style and the abilities and trustworthiness of your staff. It can help you to make proper use of your own time and talents. It can also be an important factor concerning the vital aspect of your image as presented to your clients.

However, when you are in business and totally absorbed in some fascinating new project, it is not always easy to delegate, even when you need to. For one thing, you may not immediately be in a position to offload some of your routine duties. Lack of finance or lack of expertise on the part of your staff may both play a part.

I must admit that in the early days I could not afford to pay too much attention to my image. I was too busy for one thing, wearing so many different hats – saleslady, invoice typist, advertising executive, packer, book-keeper, delivery driver, etc.

It was difficult to decide which outfit to wear when, for economic reasons, I was both delivering goods and visiting clients on the same run. I often felt like hiding my hands to conceal chipped fingernails and grime from handling parcels when I hurried up to Purchasing to see my client, direct from offloading the supplies in Goods Inwards.

It didn't look good – and I knew it!

As soon as my finances permitted, I took on a part-time delivery driver. But whenever there was an urgent delivery that could not be delegated to the driver, I would deliver it myself. One day I almost lost my client through my anxiety to give prompt service.

I carried the goods into the building (the firm did not have a Goods Inwards facility), was met by the buyer and asked him where I should deposit the parcels. I expected the usual reply. 'On the table over there', or maybe 'Let me take the top one and we'll put them straight in the stationery cupboard.'

Not a bit of it.

'Come this way,' he invited and strode along the corridor, with me trailing behind, peeping over the top of my load.

The MD happened to exit suddenly from his office, took in the situation at a glance and berated the young buyer in no uncertain terms for the 'disgraceful' way he was treating me. In principle I tended to agree with the MD. (Not just because I was a woman. I think a male visitor would be entitled to the same courtesy.) But I did not wish to lose the account over a comparatively trifling matter of thoughtlessness.

But by now my buyer was acutely embarrassed and I felt it must be the end for me. He would never order from my company again.

I chatted to him for several moments afterwards – anything to distract him from the awful incident. He did keep his business with me, but I tried from then onwards never to do my own deliveries except in the cases of direst emergency, or if I was on particularly comfortable terms with my client.

It is a good idea to have a few 'outs' if you are ever in a corner. Mine, with regard to a delivery I would prefer to leave to the driver next day, is the torn ligament in my back. As a last resort it is fairly useful, since it brooks no argument. It is, I think, quite reasonable that after proving yourself you indulge your ego a little.

If you don't *act* like the MD, you won't get *treated* like the MD.

That's not to say that you can't 'bend the rules' occasionally. On the contrary, there may be times when it is positively beneficial to you to do so.

But do make sure you get the credit.

'You need this delivery urgently? Oh dear, my driver's up north at the moment! Look, don't worry, I'll do it *myself* this afternoon for you.'

In other words, let them think that it is not at all what you're used to, but since it is for *them*, an exception can be made.

It occurred to me that maybe men instinctively know how to delegate, how to spot unwelcome situations before they occur. I put this point to an experienced woman executive, Anne Watts.

'They certainly don't know this instinctively,' she says. 'They have been actively conditioned into this by other men. Women do not normally get this sort of advice. It's the kind of thing the chaps sort out between themselves over a drink!'

20

OCCUPATIONAL HAZARDS

Whatever course you take in life, there will always be occupational hazards, i.e. those personal, unpleasant hiccups that are almost invited by the nature of your chosen area of operation. Consider the following problems:

For the Executive Secretary – Moving Up

You have been with the company for some time and your duties encompass far more than the normal secretarial skills expected of a senior secretary. You no longer take the minutes at meetings – you are far too busy participating. Your advice is sought on matters of office policy. You are responsible for taking on and controlling staff. An avid reader of the *Financial Times*, you dabble in stocks and shares in private. Yet, you are still typing letters . . .

Handling. First and foremost, you need to dispense with the 'secretary' label. You're obviously too good at it!

Could you take on even more non-secretarial duties? Could you then persuade your boss that *you* need a secretary?

Whatever you do, do not order a new typewriter for your secretary. Hand over yours. Try to find a new job title appropriate to the new role you are pursuing.

Then go after the rise your new position demands.

For the Employment Agency Proprietor

You have placed an excellent secretary with a client on a long-term temporary basis. When the engagement is completed, she works for a week or two elsewhere, then leaves you, saying she has found a permanent job.

Later you find she has misled you and that the permanent job is with the company for whom she originally worked on a long-term basis. The company has asked her to keep quiet about it, so they won't have to pay your fee for the introduction.

Handling. The only course is to challenge them. If you know who was responsible for this reprehensible piece of skulduggery, try to make contact with his/her senior.

Give this person the benefit of the doubt – he/she genuinely may not have known what was going on and may react as angrily as you at the deception. So state your case openly and honestly, but leaving them in no doubt that you are seriously aggrieved.

The chances are they will apologise and pay up, and, providing your contact deals sensibly with the party responsible, will continue to use your services.

If your contact is hostile, your only course is taking legal advice.

For the Consultancy

You are likely to spend a great deal of time away from home. You could be alone a lot. You may get so caught up in your work that you feel only half a person when you get home, exhausted and tense.

Handling. Since you can do very little about your life-style, do at least try to take regular holidays and lots of short breaks. A week at a health farm should get you back into condition.

For the Women in Charge of Men

Of course not *all* men are so offensive but when they are . . .
This is an actual case study.

'When I am in my office, I can't help but hear them. They
don't know I can hear them, but the walls are thin. Their
remarks are not only obscene, but so *nasty*. When a pretty
woman passes by the door, I am sure that sometimes she
must hear them. Sometimes I'm sure they must think all
women are deaf!

'I would like to have a wider choice of workers, but their
skills are so specialised, you have to take what you can get.'

Handling. The woman concerned simply affects not to hear
the unpleasant jibes of her workers. I did suggest to her that
she might employ one good, intelligent worker and give that
worker supervisory authority so that a reasonable standard of
behaviour could be maintained within the workshop.

For the Dealer

Owing to difficulties in servicing a certain account, you begin
to depend too heavily on your supplier for back-up. He gives
you plenty of verbal assurance and seems a nice enough guy,
so you take him with you to meet your customer to discuss
technicalities.

First chance he gets, he invites your customer to lunch
behind your back, and takes the credit for the bottle of Scotch
you sent your client at Christmas. The next thing you know
you are out on your ear.

Handling. If you decide to act as a middle-person, do not be
persuaded to introduce your supplier to your customer,
unless you are very sure of the former's reputation and ethics.
Supposing that you are in a corner, out of your depth in any
way (aren't we all from time to time?), could you find a
disinterested party to help you, someone with the specialised

knowledge that you need but whose business interests are not in competition with yours? It would be worth paying this person a consultancy fee to prevent the disruption that an unethical supplier might cause.

Never be persuaded to operate under the name of your supplier on a commission basis. Run your own show, use your own business title and send out your own delivery notes and invoices.

Otherwise you may be severely restricted in the future if you wish to change direction. In addition, you lay yourself open to backlash if your supplier tries to cut you out or if you fall out with him.

21

EMPLOYING STAFF

When you decide the climate is right to take on staff, be very careful in your choice.

A person may be loyal, likeable, neat and intelligent. At least, on the surface. But that person may also be totally unsuitable for a number of reasons. So consider what you *don't* want before deciding what you do want.

If you are a novice in the game of interviewing – and it can be fairly traumatic until you are accustomed to it – have in front of you a list of questions you would like to ask and points you wish to make. This ensures that you are in charge from the outset, that you will not be lost for words and that you do not omit to ask some vital question.

You are of course looking for someone a little bit like yourself. Someone with confidence, aptitude, flexibility and a good personality.

But you must remain objective. Remember, if your prospective employer is keen, he or she is working to put on the best performance possible. What you *aren't* looking for may be a whole lot harder to spot.

Types

The prattler

Nothing can be more time-consuming, soul-destroying and uncrushable than loquacity. Even if you have every confidence in your own ability to terrify this employee into submissive silence, your constant presence would be required to maintain such an unnatural state of existence for the persistent chatterbox. Unchecked, consider the effect of this employee upon your customers, your other staff and your telephone bill.

The hypochondriac

A predilection for self-pity is another great time-waster. This is a fatal flaw, since it will mean you will regularly be left in the lurch. Your hypochondriac may also have a tendency to loquacity – a fearsome combination. You will be equally put out whether your employee is off sick or complainingly in attendance at your office.

The obsessive

This covers any person with an abnormally high pre-occupation with an idea, e.g. pop star groupies, nymphomaniacs, egotists, anyone who thinks of himself or herself as a sex object, an evangelist, Napoleon or whatever.

Such characters will not have the inclination to give their work more than perfunctory consideration. In some cases there could be instances of negligence, damaging enough in themselves, or actual harm could be done to the company identity. One firm I know employed a delivery driver who upset a number of its customers by showing the secretaries his collection of pornographic literature.

At the Interview

When you interview your prospective employee, spend some time so that you can weigh up all these points. If you wish to impress upon the employee your need for reliability, now is the time to do so, not later.

In a small business such as my own it is essential that these points are sorted out in the beginning, as the employee is going to be critical to the smooth running of my business, e.g. *one* driver, *one* assistant to mind the office and telephones while I am out seeing clients. Therefore it is more difficult for me if an employee is unreliable than maybe for a larger company, where there are other staff who can cover for the absentee. Moreover, it saves bad feeling if everyone knows exactly where they stand.

It is helpful if you draw up a form of job description and match the type of experience, qualifications or abilities you require to the individual's characteristics. In addition, let your applicant have a written copy so that he or she is in no doubt about your expectations.

If you want to ask questions, it is a good idea to draft them out beforehand, so that you will not be distracted or go off on a tangent. This way you will maintain control over the interview.

I think it is best for both of you if you try to help your applicant to relax at the beginning of the interview. Being 'on trial' is traumatic for many people. If the applicant is quite obviously unsuitable, I like to try to let them off lightly. 'Obviously your typing is excellent, but unfortunately we do need some book-keeping experience.'

There may be occasions, however, when it is not possible to make a quick judgment. On the face of it your applicant seems OK, but somehow you're not quite sure . . .

How to Recognise Undesirable Applicants

Since, owing to nervousness, some people tend to talk too much or else be reduced to monosyllables at interviews, the prattler may not be easy to spot. On the other hand, hypochondriacs tend to be fussy people. Female hypochondriacs usually carry capacious handbags which may rattle from the countless bottles of pills contained therein. Both male and female hypochondriacs tend to nitpick.

If you have a prospective employee with whom you are fairly impressed but whom you suspect may turn out to be the prattler or the hypochondriac, arrange a second interview, if possible, in a more relaxed atmosphere, say a reception or rest area, where there is comfortable seating, maybe a couple of pot plants; and where you can have a cup of coffee in peace. This should loosen up your interviewee and give you more chance to spot any undesirable traits.

There are of course many idiosyncrasies which may not emerge at an interview, or even for some time after. However, I think the level of interest your interviewee shows in your business serves as a good guide. Does the prospective employee ask questions, not just about holidays and pay but about the nature of your business, e.g. how it operates, how wide an area it covers, how long it has been established?

Finally, unless you are very sure, don't accept the person on spec. Give yourself time to think, ask for references. If possible, get the telephone number of the interviewee's last employer and speak with this company personally. You are more likely to get the truth than by a letter or testimonial.

Tell your interviewee that you have three more candidates to see tomorrow and that you will give him or her your decision as soon as possible.

If, in spite of the above precautions, you find you have unwittingly employed the prattler, the hypochondriac or worse, and you feel you must dismiss him or her, never procrastinate, although it may be hard. People's office and social skills may improve with time and effort, but not generally their personality defects.

22

EMPLOYEES AND THE FEMALE BOSS

Human interaction within working relationships is unpredictable, but I have in the course of my own experience, noted certain fairly consistent responses.

The Older Male Employee

The older man tends to try to diffuse what might seem to him an awkward situation by the frequent use of terms of endearment, addressing one as dear, darling or pet. He may never use your proper name. If this bothers you, you will have to tell him about it, but it is notoriously difficult to change the habits of persons of a certain age.

On the plus side older people are often more conscientious and concerned than the young, stay put longer and have no axe to grind in competing with you.

The Older Female Employee

The older woman may attempt to mother you. This may be irritating at times, but she will probably do her utmost to ensure you are not troubled by trivialities. She may pop into the Post Office for you on her way to work, dust the stock or even repair the skirt you snagged. Do appreciate whatever she does outside the line of duty, but avoid becoming too obligated. It is pretty difficult to reprimand someone for a messily typed letter if they have spent the best part of last Saturday afternoon searching their local haberdashers for a button to replace the one missing from your best suede jacket.

Younger Employees

Younger people are naturally more acclimatised to the idea of equality, and, provided they have been carefully selected and are both willing and able, should not pose too many problems directly related to the woman boss/employee relationship. They may be a little wary of you at first, but do not confuse sullenness with shyness.

Younger poeple learn more quickly than older and are more receptive to new ideas. Therefore you will spend less time trying to persuade them to unlearn bad habits or other ideas which do not suit your system.

Employees of a Similar Age Group

Your contemporaries are likely to be far more critical of you and your methods than other employees. It may be that they have useful suggestions to make, but if you do not agree, stick roundly to your principles and objectives.

It is probable that this employee could feel much more at liberty to oppose you, as a woman, than your counterpart male. This may be because some women bosses find it unnerving to face unpopularity, and if this is your weakness, it is one that you must overcome if you are to progress and win.

[116]

Remember, if being loved is *too* important to you, your employee will sense that you are a soft touch and your directives will be accordingly less effective.

Discrimination

Before I started running my own business, I once attended an interview for employment as secretary to a woman solicitor. The secretary whose job was to become vacant interviewed me on her boss's behalf.

'Do you mind working for a woman?' she asked. The question was not a casual one, but asked under positive instruction from the professional woman herself.

Many women I have talked to have expressed their preference for working for a man and many men their abhorrence at the thought of a woman boss. I suppose one cannot tell people what they must and must not like, but it does seem an anomaly that employers must not discriminate sexually yet employees certainly can and do.

In short, you may not have as wide a choice of employees as your male counterpart.

Protecting Your Interests

Some employees may be young enough, old enough and smart enough to pose a threat to you if they are so inclined. For instance, with the inside knowledge of how your company operates, could the super negotiator or salesperson you have just engaged decide to set up in business half a mile from your premises and acquire a proportion of your clientele to boot?

Protect yourself with a properly drafted, legally approved contract to help prevent this. Maintain a sensible degree of personal contact with your key accounts and watch carefully for any warning signs.

23

TRAINING STAFF

A businessman I know always says, with regard to training staff, 'Any member of staff is entitled to have a new task explained to them three times. If after three times they still haven't got it, then the job is beyond their capability.'

As a general rule, this maxim probably works quite well for him. I, personally, have found exceptions. Some people are slow developers; maybe they lack confidence, which can create a nervous mental block. Persons may be slow to learn, but once they have it, they have it forever and will be meticulous in the execution of their duties.

A lot of it is to do with caring. If an employee *wants* to learn, *wants* to do a good job, then you are halfway there. It might be better to make an effort with an employee like this than to take on someone quick and careless, who might leave you at the drop of a hat.

As an employer, I can cope with genuine mistakes. What I abhor is negligence.

I had an assistant once who was really quite clever, but unpunctual. She did not live very far, yet she was always late. She would rush into the office, hot and flustered and full of apologies.

One day I had to go to town and leave her in charge of the office. 'Please don't be late tomorrow,' I told her. 'There is no one else here to answer the telephone.'

She was to cover the office in the morning, leave a lunchtime message on the answerphone (saying the office was closed for lunch but would open at 2 pm) and get back in time for the afternoon session.

I had never intended to try to catch her out. But I finished my business in town much earlier than expected and was back in my office by lunchtime.

Twenty-five minutes late she sauntered into the office. She had all the time in the world because she thought I wasn't there. Her manner changed when she saw me there.

The apologies were profuse, the excuses watertight. Maybe I could have forgiven her if she had rushed in, hot and flustered, as she usually did. It was her slow, easy unconcern that floored me.

She was only concerned with keeping me sweet in order to keep her job. She was not at all bothered about me keeping my customers. She did not care about doing a good job.

Such experiences with employees *are* galling, especially when you know you have been fair and flexible with them. Obviously, in larger organisations, the hierarchy does take care of many such aberrations, but in a small company each employee must motivate him/herself.

Training new people is incredibly time-consuming. They are going to make lots of mistakes and need constant supervision. Don't ever assume knowledge unless your employee has come to you with specific qualifications. It is so easy to take certain matters for granted when you know your own business inside out. For instance, there is no point in getting annoyed with your new office junior for not filing away the statements if the poor kid doesn't know what a statement's supposed to look like. 'If you don't understand something I tell you, don't be afraid to ask', is a more helpful reaction than 'Good grief! I thought *everyone* knew that!'

When you explain a new task to trainees, don't only tell them how. Tell them *why*. Tell them what happens next. If someone knows *why* they are doing something, they are in a much better position to sort out problems, thus saving you time. (I never bothered with algebra at school. I couldn't see the point in all those silly equations. If someone had explained to me something about their application, I would have been much more interested.)

So, to summarise: knowing *why* you are doing something makes a person more interested in both the application and the result, makes the job more worthwhile and helps the trainee to operate with greater efficiency.

When you have found a good, reliable employee, show him/her that you trust them and give them more responsibility. Reassure them if you have to check their work. 'You've done this very well. You don't mind if I just check it over, do you? It's so easy to slip up on the final analysis. I know, because I've done it myself.'

In larger set-ups it is probably a good idea to train one exemplary employee until that person is completely au fait with your methods, then ask him or her to help the others.

If an employee is good in most areas and dependable, but has a weak area that bothers you, it might be a good idea to encourage a course at evening school, or possibly even suggest 'day-release' so that he/she can attend college.

A final word on training people from Anne Watts.

'I would like to suggest the advisability of educating your male assistants – they can be a great asset.

'To demonstrate:

'Male assistant, Chris Stephens, and his female manager Carol Greaves were visiting thirty administration managers in N. England. This is how the introductions were handled:

'Carol Greaves: "May I introduce Chris Stephens and his team."

'Chris Stephens: "Thank you for the introduction and elevation – and may I, in turn, introduce my manager Carol Greaves."

'The administration managers grovelled for the entire lunch!'

24

COMPUTERS – WILL YOU WANT ONE? DO YOU NEED ONE?

You may love or hate the idea of owning a computer (no one is indifferent) but one thing is for sure – computers are here to stay. Even if you opt out of installing your own, you are bound to be plagued by other people's.

The Advantages of Owning a Computer

1 A useful scapegoat

The enlightened know that when a computer malfunctions, there is a 99 per cent chance that it is due to operator error, or even programmer error. Nevertheless computers are invariably blamed when something goes amiss. After all, at the present level of technology, the business computer cannot verbally contradict you as you are lying into your 'phone.

2 A useful go-between

Computers dealing with ledger programmes don't consult their human 'masters' at all. They write cosy, informal letters to one another, tactfully suggesting that if the overdue amount for February is paid within the next 7 days, it will not be necessary to advise the boss, Mr Credit Controller. These matey missives usually close with the following: 'Why should we involve *him*. Please send me your cheque and we'll forget all about it'.

So computers do supply a sort of business social service, allowing people to save face, defusing potential explosions, permitting the ultimate 'climb-down'.

'Oh dear, did you get one of *those* letters,' you tell your irate customer. 'Don't worry about it, the computer sends them out automatically after 21 days. Of course we all know, here in the office, the reasons why you are holding back invoice no. xxxxxx.'

3 Time-saving

Give proper consideration to the amount of time you spend on your paperwork. If it is less than 5 or 6 hours a week, you do not need the hassle of owning a computer. If it is more, you may benefit, and after the inevitable teething troubles, the mishaps, tantrums, puzzles and various other traumas, the computer will begin to save you time, providing you have learned how to use it to its full potential.

The Disadvantages of Owning a Computer

1 Incompatibility

You are human. It is unbending and, except in cases of electrical malfunction or a power cut, infallible. It records unforgivingly all your mistakes and all the subsequent mistakes you make trying to put the first mistakes right. It also has an irritating habit of bleeping at you angrily when you accidentally put in an invalid option. At times, you will long for an analysis pad and a bottle of Tippex.

2 Malfunction

When it is good, it is very very good. When it is bad, it is horrid. Just like the little girl in the childhood nursery rhyme, a malfunctioning computer is a diabolical headache. If you have not backed up (i.e. duplicated) your discs, you lose all your data and have to start again.

To summarise, *always*:

(a) Remember that a computer is an exacting and demanding baby. To reap the benefits, you must first put in the effort to ensure you have the right programmes for your business requirements and that you understand all the implications. This is not necessarily as difficult as it sounds, but does require the investment of time and the correct training.

(b) Keep your back-up (copy) discs elsewhere, away from the machine, especially if you are hoping for an Act of God that will do away with the computer and enable you to claim the insurance. You can then run your back-up discs on someone else's machine and copy the printouts into a nice, friendly accounts book.

25

STATUS SYMBOLS AND WOMEN

If prestige is important to you, and it is to many people, then you may find the aspects of status that have their roots in material things more difficult to enjoy. Women do not seem to attract equal prestige from traditionally male-orientated status symbols. (This would not of course apply to a woman whose achievements were well known. But in the case of ordinary working women the general assumption seems to be that there must be a man in the background, doing all the brainwork!)

Once, in the car park of a mutual acquaintance, I met a salesman who worked for a competitor of my company. I had just acquired my first brand-new car, a sleek and racy affair with silver, metallic paint.

'It's all right for you,' he muttered disparagingly. '*I* have to buy my *own* cars.'

I blinked and stared despairingly at my lovely new baby. There it languished, its paint a little duller, reduced to mere unearned income, the folly of an over-generous boss or an indulgent husband.

Oh well! The only possible defence is to maintain a sense of humour and turn the tables by making a joke out of the situation.

However, when I acquired my first computer, eyes did start to pop a little. My business could no longer be regarded as a male-dominated concern, for the simple reason that I had put everybody right on that point. The acquisition of a piece of equipment costing £3,000 to process my accounts finally dispelled the cottage-industry image.

So next time you see a man proving he is the most powerful hunter in the pack as he sits in his high-back executive leather chair, behind his large double-pedestal antique desk, absent-mindedly flicking his cigar ash over his secretary's shoe, make yourself a promise. Promise yourself you will *never* be intimidated by the power games that men play. If you are, you will always be a secretary with ash on her shoe.

26

YOUR PERSONAL CREDIBILITY AND THE RESPONSES OF OTHERS

Whether I am doing particularly well or not, I have various stock answers to questions about the state of my business affairs. If the enquirer is influential to my business, I tell him exactly what I think he ought to hear.

Clients

Generally speaking, my business is neither extremely good nor desperately bad. Sometimes I have a run of good luck, but it was usually preceded by a couple of low months. On the other hand, it might be that last week was not too good but since Tuesday it has definitely picked up. In principle, I do not allow my customers to think me too poor, thus indicating I am not too hot at my job; nor do I insinuate that I am chuckling all the way to the bank. This is important for the following reasons:

(a) They may decide you are charging too much and start watching your invoices.
(b) You may invoke their jealousy and subsequent alienation.

I know a businessman who owns a Mercedes but does his

sales calls in a Ford Sierra. (None of the above applies to the United States, where it is not normally considered criminal to be successful.)

Suppliers

A different approach is required for suppliers. One must at all times be doing exceedingly well. The better your business, the bigger the discounts allowed and the more efficient the service provided.

If the business you place with them is modest, drop a few dark hints about orders you place with their competitors. This should make them keener to please you. If you give any indication that you are not doing as well as expected, credit control may tighten like a noose around your neck.

Staff

Once again we have the old problem of envy. Always remember that when the business goes through a bad patch, it will be you who will:

(a) Stop taking holidays.

(b) Lie awake at night, tossing and turning.

(c) Reduce your salary by one-third.

(d) Perm your own hair.

Human nature being what it is, most people will forget all about this, will bitch about the business lunches you enjoy and grumble about other trappings of success which they consider you don't deserve. They will grumble not to you but to each other and to other people.

There is not much you can do about this, except set yourself above it and refuse to be drawn. The following procedures are useful.

(a) Have a special drawer in your filing cabinet where you keep your bank statements and restaurant bills safely under lock and key.

(b) During profitable periods do not be pressured into giving rises which exceed the market rate for the job. You won't be able to take them away in 3 months' time, when your Number One client has gone into liquidation with 2 months' invoices owing! (If you want to show appreciation for hard work and improve staff morale, a one-off bonus or maybe a party might be a good idea.)

(c) Try not to confide too much in your staff unless you are sure they are trustworthy.

Coping with Envy from Business Associates

In my experience there seems to be one sure way of recognising envy, whether it comes at you over the telephone or by direct confrontation. Most people can control the words they utter and many can control their facial expressions. Fewer can handle their timing.

If you want to find out just who isn't too happy about your success, watch out for . . . the long drawn-out silence – that terribly painful pause that goes on just a fraction too long after you have imparted your bit of good news, e.g.

'Oh, by the way Mary, I've just found out I've been promoted to the Board (or been accepted by Mensa, or had my new project approved/thesis accepted for publication)'
Then follows – the long drawn-out silence.
'Oh really, how terrific for you. I'm so pleased . . .'

The disparaging remarks don't come till a little later. Often they will be subtle. Nevertheless the intention is to trivialise your achievement.

- 'You're on the *Board*. I heard they were talking to a few people. Finally managed to pressgang *you*, did they!'

- 'So you got in! At last! Full marks for even trying!'

- 'How much did that cost you?'

Don't waste too much time feeling hurt. That's negative. Just treasure your friends – those who tell you how pleased they are, without having to steel themselves before gushing approval.

Nevertheless I think it is quite a useful way of finding out just who your allies are. The more you know about your adversaries, the more power you have . . . !

Outsiders

It is not their concern, so don't elucidate if you do not wish to. However, it is satisfying to have a few quick answers to take care of any put-downs. A modest statement with a sting in the tail often does the trick. When someone makes a disparaging remark about your 'pin-money' or about 'cottage industries', just say, airily: 'It's only a small one-woman business. In fact this is the first year my turnover has gone into six figures.'

If someone suggests it might be easier for you if you got yourself a little typing job, answer,
'I do so agree with you. But I'd feel awful about sacking all the staff just to relieve the pressure.'

As one of my friends pointed out recently, isn't it funny how women often seem to be looking out for a *little* job? Men, even if they are roadsweepers, *always* have important *big* jobs. Only women ever have *little* jobs.

Patronising and singularly unpleasant innuendoes may surface because you work from home. Regardless of the fact that many successful business*men* work from home without any aspersions being cast on their status, when a woman works from home, it's somehow *quite* different.

Try turning the situation inside out: 'I decided to convert the back of the house into offices. Of course it was a terrible battle getting planning permission, but it's so pleasant looking out on to the shrubbery while you work. I do concede that it would have been cheaper and easier simply to rent premises and have done with it, but I've never regretted the additional financial outlay.'

Never allow anyone to make you uncomfortable because of something you don't have, whatever the reason you don't have it. Just murmur mysteriously, 'Of course, I've thought about it. After all, in the light of our general overheads, it's a minor consideration, but I'm not sure it's the right thing for me at the moment.'

Get the picture?

27

THE RIGHT PRODUCT

Unless you have kissed the blarney stone, your future success is, to a degree, dependent upon the desirability and availability of your product.

Dealers and middle-women selling off-the-shelf products do not normally encounter this problem, since their clients have a choice of brands and types. The dealer's goal is to sell himself and his service against the competition. However, if your company is in manufacturing, your product must be tried and tested before you commit yourself totally.

Another of my enterprises before I started my office-supplies business was in 'fashion' pendants. At that time Disney-type decorations were much in evidence. People sported Goofies, Mickey Mouses, Pink Elephants and Little Pigs on their jeans, jackets, sweaters and holdalls. I decided to cash in on this new trend.

I arranged for some large, perspex, smoke-coloured discs to be cut and hole-punched, bought aluminium chains in bulk to hang them on, then on each disc I stuck a caricature featuring some lovable baby animal. Finally, armed with my samples, I trundled around to several famous department stores and convinced the buyers that this was the ultimate in teenage fashion jewellery.

They sold like hot cakes.

The next week I popped into the two stores where I had sold the most pendants, just to check out if it was time for a fresh supply. I counted the pendants that still remained. One store had made a sale. One pendant!

Three weeks later no more had moved. Six weeks later they were marked down to half-price. The final degradation came shortly after. They had been taken from the display stand and piled into a cardboard box with 10p each Final Reduction marked on the front.

OK, so it was a rotten idea! I could never make that second call on my buyers unless I found something new and absolutely watertight to offer, plus the nerve to face them after I had, though innocently, so misled them.

It was, however, good experience for me, and ironically quite a confidence booster. If I could sell an uncommercial idea like that, what could I do if I had something good to offer?

28

FAULTY GOODS AND FAULTY PEOPLE

Put It in Writing

This comes down to basic self-preservation.

While branded goods found to be defective should be replaced by your supplier without question, goods manufactured *by* or *for* your company for resale to your client are a different matter.

Bespoke items hold many hazards for the unwary, and no doubt both your client and your supplier will consider themselves absolved from all responsibility, unless you take precautions. They may not even blame you, but it is neither comfortable nor safe to be piggy-in-the-middle while they are blaming each other. As intermediary, you are answerable to both parties.

REMEMBER THAT PERSONAL BIAS IS NOTORIOUS FOR SHORTENING MEMORIES. Therefore:

(a) Issue instructions in full detail in writing, in triplicate if necessary, to your supplier to absolve you from blame at a later stage. Don't file your copy in 'Miscellaneous'. You may need to find it quickly later.

(b) Get a detailed order from your client *before* the work begins.

(c) If appropriate, provide a sample or proof for your

client's approval and obtain a signature for it. If you have a set of 'Terms and Conditions' for your company, hand him/her a copy with the sample.

Rush Jobs

'SHALL I RUSH YOUR RUSH JOB BEFORE I RUSH THE RUSH JOB I WAS RUSHING BEFORE YOU RUSHED IN.'

A poster proclaiming the above occupies a prominent position in an art studio I visit.

To the punter, his job is the most important one, the *only* one. Why then, when the job goes badly wrong, is there *always* time to send it back and wait for a remake?

Customers put much unnecessary pressure on their suppliers. There have been many 'rush jobs' discovered by a suppliers' salesperson lying unpacked and forgotten in a corner of an office or factory corridor, sometimes weeks after delivery.

Therefore there will be occasions when circumstances may preclude fully exercising the safeguards of written instructions and sampling – e.g. the job that is needed yesterday, the last-minute changes requested by the client when the job is scheduled to begin (i.e. verbal instructions which over-ride the written order).

Let us assume a quantity of model 521s have disintegrated, and your client is hopping mad. He says the adhesive is not to specification. Refer to 'The Hell Raiser' on p. 46, then proceed as follows.

If you are not sure who is at fault, tell him you will return to your office and investigate and 'phone him back tomorrow. Even if you think you might know who is at fault, tell him you will return to your office and investigate. (You need time to think, work out the best strategy for your own salvation.) Do not on any account accept responsibility at this stage, however loudly he bawls at you. If you do, it will only make it impossible to change course later on if you have made an unwise admission.

If He's Right

He can't be completely exonerated, because he shouldn't have rushed you in the first place. But you don't want to alienate him if he is likely to give you further business.

Gently point out that you were anxious to meet his deadline, so you (or your supplier) had to make the decision to get in some adhesive from a local company instead of waiting 3 weeks for it to be sent down from the regular supplier in the Outer Hebrides.

Never make too many excuses, for this will only weaken your case.

Be pragmatic if you are trying to pass the buck. Do not give the impression you are evading the issue. Your client is dealing with *you*, not your supplier, quality controller or secretary.

At best he may assist you in salvaging the situation by compromise. At worst you've lost out on this deal, this time, but you will retain the business if he is prepared to accept you have his best interests at heart.

If He's Wrong

If he's wrong, don't turn it into a witchhunt, but make one or two comments to indicate that the information with which you were furnished left something to be desired. This could give him the opportunity to pass the buck on to someone else in his company, thus saving face, or if he is big enough, to climb down gracefully and exonerate you. The best way to sort it out is by co-operation, so once you have him on your side, you must play it by ear.

If He's Wrong and You Both Know It, but He Won't Admit It

A delicate situation! He is the customer and he probably has the power, especially if he has a large company behind him.

If the loss of his business will be detrimental to you in the future, accept that, although life should be fair, it isn't. Write the whole thing off to experience and be cautious in your future dealings with him and his company.

Alternatively, if you feel very badly about the whole incident and your company can manage without his business (existing and potential), then be firm with him, send him a bill, and if he doesn't pay, instruct your solicitor. You will feel better for it.

There have been a few occasions when I have taken a hard line with a client, and after a brief lull the business has come back to me. But this will not happen if you allow the negotiations to become acrimonious. Most people will eventually forgive you if you insist they have been mistaken. But if you imply that they are liars and cheats, or bald-headed old twits, they are likely to hold it against you.

29

SCRUPLES!

By now you should be getting the picture. When it comes right down to hard cash, an awful lot of people don't have any (scruples, I mean). It might be helpful to learn to recognise the following types. They are not uncommon.

The Opportunist

'It isn't at all what we wanted. We don't think we ought to pay. Still, we might as well use them. They're no good to you, after all.'

Don't ever fall for this one. Not only do you lose out on this deal, you forfeit any profit you should enjoy on the remake. In any case it is dangerous to set a precedent like this. Once I gave in on such a matter and was subsequently subjected to much hyper-criticism from the client with a view to more free 'scrap jobs'.

Invent a good reason why he can't keep the scrap job. Your reputation is at stake, the materials can be cut down/modified/recycled. But don't let him get away with it.

The Perfectionist

'It isn't at all what we wanted. Do it again.'

Well, perhaps the job genuinely cannot be used or perhaps he is being pedantic. This is where the evidence you have on file is most needed. (Remember to put 10 per cent extra on the next rush job he gives you).

The Compromiser

'It isn't what we wanted, but we'd feel better about it if you knock a bit off.'

If you or your supplier are in the wrong, you will probably have to give him a reasonable discount, appropriate in size to the degree of defectiveness and how loudly he shouts. But consider first, is it cheaper to replace it? Do not be so anxious to compensate that the sum you are left with is less than the profit you would have made if you simply replaced the job. This could easily be the case if tooling or origination charges were incurred in the original costing but not in the repeat run.

Your Supplier

He may insist that the model 521s that disintegrated in your client's warehouse were perfectly A1 when they were collected from his factory. 'Your client's warehouse must be damp. Are you sure there's not a leak in the roof?' Maybe eventually he'll accept some or all of the responsibility, especially since you were waving a fully detailed order under his nose, specifying the type of adhesive required.

But if you think customers are tricky, be warned that suppliers pose an equal threat. Since it is in their interests to keep you happy, their methods of screwing you down will tend to be more devious unless:

(a) Your business is so worthwhile and profitable that he/she accepts responsibility without question. ('Possible, but if this happens you are probably paying too highly for his/her services anyway.)

(b) He or she is so thoroughly honest that he/she would not dream of taking unfair advantage of you.
(Highly unlikely!)

Human nature being what it is, the supplier may decide to put an extra 10 per cent on all future work from you to make good his/her loss. Be one step ahead. Get estimates from the supplier *and* his/her competitors.

Make your supplier quote every time against a check quote and let him/her know what you are doing. Even if you do not have time to check, you need not let him/her know it. This is important, for if your supplier gets into the habit of loading your prices, he/she may continue to do so long after they have been compensated.

When the Buck Stops with You

Obviously there will be times you will have to accept the blame for your own error. (You left the model 521s in the van overnight with the windows open and there was a thunderstorm. That was why the adhesive did not harden properly.)

To do this impersonally and fatalistically must be one of the most difficult business lessons to learn. However, it is quite normal practice for manufacturers to incorporate a scrap charge in their costing system, so why not operate in the same way? If you add an extra 2.5% when pricing, you will feel better when a catastrophe does occur, and it will alleviate the drain on your annual profit margin.

[140]

If you are operating in a cut-price market, as many of us are these days, you could instead levy a larger scrap charge on to the 'urgent' accounts. (After all, having waited at the factory till late Monday night for the machine to disgorge the model 521s for the client's panic deadline of 8 am Tuesday morning, you were fed up, starving and exhausted. Otherwise you would never have been so careless as to leave the consignment exposed to the elements in a windowless van.)

In my experience there are few individual 'urgent' jobs, just simply well organised accounts and muddled, last-minute accounts. Errors do occur more frequently when people who panic are concerned. You are better advised to risk losing their work through higher prices than continually to scrap jobs and try to justify the service they receive against profits.

Then you can remain competitive for your desirable accounts.

30

DOUBLE-TALK

People generally use a great deal of double-talk, either because they wish to disguise what they mean or because they prefer to deceive themselves into believing they don't mean what they do mean. Confused? Read on . . .

He carved me up means either:

(a) He used dishonest means to make a gain to my disadvantage.

(b) The other guy got the contract and I'm furious about it.

I used strategy means:

(a) I got where I wanted through my devious manipulation of the other party.

(b) I got the contract and I'm jolly pleased with myself.

He's got verbal diarrhoea can mean:

(a) He talks too much.

(b) Verbally I am unable to outwit him.

Before I commit myself I have to refer it to the board/my MD/my accountant may mean just that, but more likely explanations are:

(a) I need more time to think.

(b) I'm afraid to make decisions all by myself.

(c) I've already decided to place the business/job/promotion elsewhere but I haven't the clout to admit it to your face.

You're looking particularly attractive today means: 'You're putting me in a corner. I know you're after the business/ promotion/job but I need more time to think before I make a decision.'

You play ball with me and I'll play ball with you means one of the following:

(a) I'm not a big shot by a long way and I'd like to be a big shot, so I rely on psychological blackmail.

(b) You can offer me a lot more than I can offer you.

(c) I can offer you a lot more than you may suspect. What are you doing tonight?

I'm sorry but something's come up that cannot be avoided. Our lunchdate/meeting/other important appointment will have to be postponed: How about?

(a) The bailiffs have just walked in.

(b) The taxman found out about my other bank account.

(c) I've just cracked it with my secretary and we're popping back to her place for the afternoon.

Please give my proposal your serious consideration. If you don't, you're losing money means simply: 'If you don't, I'll lose money'.

Weeee. . .ll, I'm afraid this is rather a grey area means:

(a) I don't know but I don't want you to know I don't know.

(b) I can't make a decision but I don't want you to know I can't make a decision.

31

PAYMENTS

I have aimed this section primarily at the woman employed in an executive capacity in a small company and the woman who runs her own firm. Most larger concerns will already be operating established methods of credit control, to which the following may not apply.

The Middle Person

No doubt you will find your suppliers will take a much tougher line with you Small Fry than you are able to adopt with your clients, on whom you have been working to woo and charm them away from your competitors, and who you are naturally reluctant to upset with clumsy demands and veiled threats. Your supplier will probably allow you the standard 30 days nett monthly account (i.e. payment at the end of the month following the month of invoice) or even 2–3 weeks longer if that is the firm's usual practice. When this period has elapsed, the supplier will:

1 Send you curt chase-up letters.

2 Stop your supplies.

3 If your payment is still not forthcoming, the supplier will send you a stiffer letter, perhaps via a debt collector.

4 You may then receive a Notice of Legal Action.

5 At the end of the time specified on the Notice the supplier may summons you.

You could forestall the above train of events if, knowing that you have sufficient sums owing to you to settle, you make a call to your supplier's Bought Ledger, explaining the difficulties regarding your cash flow, assuring that department it has only occurred because your slowest paying client wished to use up his budget before the end of his company's financial year, and saying when you expect to be able to pay. A part payment to show good faith would be well received at this stage.

The supplier should be sympathetic. On a larger scale, he or she can identify with your problem.

The Agency

If you are dealing in people, not goods, the pressures upon you will be even greater. Staff will not be interested in excuses, they must be paid on the dot.

If you habitually pay the wages on Thursday but, owing to unforeseen circumstances, delay payment until Friday, you may have a mutiny on your hands. I once saw it happen, and I never realised before how many people spend Thursday evenings late-night shopping at Sainsbury's. Coincidentally, all these people, although high-wage earners, had not a bite left to eat in their fridges and freezers!

Staff will have to be paid weeks before you are able to obtain settlement from your clients, and you will certainly need an overdraft to lean on at times. Be sure to include the cost of this in your pricing system.

Credit Control

Whatever the nature of your business, you must keep on top of credit control. If you are running a small business, either for yourself or as an employee, you will be operating on a personal level and against fierce competition, making the usual methods of credit control difficult, if not impossible. Do not despair. *Use* this personal affiliation you have cultivated with your clients. I suspect it is one of the best procedures anyway, for many people respond more readily to the personal approach, and I know I succeed in influencing my customers to pay promptly where male associates seem to experience difficulty.

In the first instance don't send letters, and keep it light. Make a telephone call to your client's Bought Ledger and, if possible, promote friendly relations with the influential people in this department. You could try:

- 'I wonder if we could receive payment for April please?'

- 'Could I give you a small jog about the April account?'

You see, friendly and not too pushy. People will respond in one of the following ways:

- 'It will be in the post tonight.'

- 'I'll deal with it next week.'

- 'I can't do anything at the moment. Our cheques need two directors' signatures and one's in New York.'

- 'I'll look into it.'

- 'It went in the post last night.'

- 'You can ask, but that doesn't mean you'll get it. You'll just have to join the queue like everyone else.'

[147]

If the response is co-operative, thank your contact and tell him/her how grateful you are. If your contact seems unconcerned, dispense with subtlety and have a word with your buyer. 'I wonder if you could help speed up my cheque. My cash flow is serious at the moment.'

You have already offered and maintained a super service, maybe taken him to lunch, chatted to him about his kids and his holidays. In heaven's name, he *owes* you! What can he do but agree to have words with Bought Ledger.

Still no joy one week later?

Tell your buyer that your main suppliers are cutting off your supplies in 2 days' time. (They probably are, but, if not, tell him that anyway.) You won't be able to supply him with his (think of something particularly necessary to the running of his business that you supply and that he cannot get elsewhere in a hurry). You would not be able to use this ploy on a small amount of money, as it would sound ridiculous, but it should be a reliable lever for anything in the region of several hundred pounds or more.

Apart from the possibility that he would not wish his business dealings with you to be disrupted, he should see your predicament and act immediately. The beauty of this approach is that you can imply the stopping of his supplies without hostility, since you have passed the buck on to a third party, your own supplier.

A staff agency could use a modified version of this approach. What could be more heart-rending than not having sufficient funds in the bank to pay the hardworking staff's wages on Friday? If your strategy fails to produce a result, perhaps your client is in difficulties financially. This requires ACTION:

- Stop his supplies immediately.

- Inform your debt collector or your solicitor.

Your chances of being paid will decrease as time elapses and other creditors start putting in their claims. The Bank, the

Inland Revenue, and HM Customs and Excise all have preference over you, as do the staff employed by him.

There are other methods you may use in the course of normal business accounting. The following rubber stamps are fun, can be bought from large stationers and draw attention to your monthly statements.

Reproduced by courtesy of Mark C. Brown & Son Ltd, Hull

There was a period when I was extremely busy and lapsed somewhat on credit control. My secretary and I composed the following verse and sent it to accounts which had fallen behind. It is not great poetry, does not scan properly, but we did get paid that month.

> We write to you straight from the heart
> No badwill do we wish to impart
> For your business we value a lot
> But you see, we are in quite a spot.
>
> Our suppliers have cut our supplies
> Despite all our pleas and our sighs

[149]

If you send us a cheque
We can say 'What the heck'
And dry all the tears from our eyes.

To summarise the point we raise
Your monthly cheque in THIRTY DAYS – PLEASE
(AND – WE COULD EAT EVERY DAY!)

One of the benefits of being a woman in business, as you may deduce from the points made in this chapter, is that you can break a few rules, flout convention. Convention in business is a man-made restriction. Men's hands are tied in many areas, for old traditions die hard and accepted procedures are seldom questioned.

Since we women have not been around business long enough to understand these deeper mysteries, all sorts of allowances that are not made for men are made for us. This gives our sex a decided advantage.

32

LIQUIDATIONS

There can of course be disadvantages in growing larger. A smaller business is in essence more manageable, as it is simpler to keep tabs on things. The larger you become, the sharper you need to be to keep control – that is until you are large enough to employ the best people to do this for you. In the meantime, remember, the higher you rise, the harder you fall.

A bad debt that is 10 per cent of your turnover when it levels at around £2,000 per month might be less psychologically disturbing than a loss of 10 per cent of £9,000 per month. However, it is more likely that when your turnover hits £9,000 per month, your bad debt could be a much larger proportion than 10 per cent.

The reason for this is that when you first start, the load of debts is likely to be spread. You are building your clientele and diversifying in order to do so. Probably several companies are trying you out, placing a small amount of their business your way to see how you handle it.

As time goes by you may become tempted to pay the most attention to those clients who are the most profitable and responsive to you. Thus you may come to depend upon fewer of your clients for most of your business, even maybe only one or two.

This is a dangerous but easy trap to fall into.

These are the danger signals that a client may be in financial difficulty:

1 Word of mouth. The grapevine within your trade may be more reliable than you think. KEEP TUNED IN.

2 They have paid regularly on the 14th of the month following the month of invoice for the first 18 months. Then they start paying on the last day of the month. Gradually their payments get later and later and later . . .

3 Where they previously ordered forty packs or fifty of your product each time, they suddenly start ordering one pack at a time. Then they ask if you will split a pack for them.

However, by far the best method of getting the feel of your client's financial situation is by close personal contact. One of my buyers once warned me that his company was in difficulties and advised me to set a credit limit. This I did, as a calculated gamble, thinking it would be worth this reduced risk to be around if and when they recovered.

Yet I did make a serious error of judgement, mostly due to ignorance. After a bad summer season their business began to improve considerably, or so it seemed. I made my customary personal contacts, checked the stock levels and action in the warehouse, noted the increase in staff and factory workers employed – and stopped worrying.

The Bank foreclosed on them just after their winter peak had finished.

In retrospect I can see it was logical. The Bank, cunningly allowed the bad season to pass, since it would stand a better chance of recovering its money by putting in the Official Receiver *after* my client's normal winter peak.

When the Receiver goes into a company, whether he is called in by the Bank or the Creditors, he has priorities in making his payments. First he looks after the Bank, then the Inland Revenue and the Customs and Excise. In other words, all the poor people who couldn't possibly manage without the money! Then come the Secured Creditors and the Staff (who may well have been responsible for the company's demise, although not always). The remainder, if any, is then shared proportionately among the poor old unsecured Creditors (you and me, the suppliers of goods and services).

Don't ask me why it's like this. It's unfair, but what do you expect when men for the most part are running things!

Anyhow, the Receiver continues to run the business to see if it can be saved, which usually it cannot, and tries to collect the debts. His fees, however, erode any benefits which might have been gained from the collection of debts.

A Creditors' Meeting must be called by law, at which time a Statement of Affairs is issued to show how your money has been squandered and at which the Directors must be present to answer your questions and provide a target for your abuse, depending upon your tolerance level and how much money you have lost. At this meeting it is decided if the Receivership may continue and for how long. If there is still a lot of money to collect, the Creditors may allow it to continue for a stipulated period.

Finally, the liquidator is called in to bury the bones, i.e. dispose of all remaining assets, and of course by this time the company has ceased to trade and possibly the goodwill has been sold at the best possible price. If you are fortunate, you may be allowed to buy back some of your stock at a reduced price. It is wise to stake your claim in writing as early on in the proceedings as possible.

If the company has been sold as a going concern, with staff being retained, it is possible but not probable that debts, or parts thereof, may be honoured. In this case you may be made an offer, which it may behove you and other creditors to accept as the lesser of two evils. Subsequently you may continue to do business with the new, it is to be hoped profitable company.

Supplying the Receivership

Goods supplied to the Receiver, providing they are backed up with a written order signed by the Receiver, are guaranteed for payment. Whatever your loss, the signed order from the Receiver is the safest business deal you will ever make.

I have only had one serious experience of dealing with the Receiver in all my years in business, so I cannot say if this is typical, but I was able to recoup one-third of my loss by charging inflated prices for the goods I supplied him. Any quotes I gave, however outrageous, were accepted (the Receiver, after all, may not be au fait with your service or product) and eventually orders were arriving without any prices whatsoever.

My biggest problem was in agonising over how far I could go in increasing my prices before I frightened them off, and towards the end of the Receivership I was naturally able to take greater risks in my charging. No wonder the Bank, that most preferential of Creditors didn't quite get all its money back, for I suspect I was not the only one amongst the 'Unsecured Creditors' who used cunning to better their 'last in the queue' situation.

PRESSURE

To counter pressure you need to relax. It does not take a genius to figure this out, yet many ignore this simple truth at their peril. Executive businessmen know the value of relaxation – hence the days off for golf, which provides in one package the three great tension relievers, good exercise, a change of scenery and pleasurable activity.

It is not so easy for a woman, especially if there is a home and family to consider. At one time I worked especially hard, and at around 5.30 each day I would be rushing back from town to cook a meal and then to process the day's work. There was no time for relaxation, for painting my fingernails or reading a novel.

Finally, in a kind of stupor, I remarked, 'The daffodils are late this year.'

'They've been and gone, dear,' explained a long-suffering friend.

I had missed the daffodils! Each day I was so busy and preoccupied that I had walked down my garden path and never even noticed them.

I decided I would never miss the daffodils again.

Hints for Gaining Time to Look at Daffodils

- When finances permit, get yourself a daily woman or, if applicable, a childminder.

- Families tend to take each other for granted. Start as you mean to go on. If you act like a slave, you will be treated like a slave.

- Keep lists of things to do. For mine I have a small manuscript book, in which I log everything, business, personal and domestic, and I tick off each item as it is dealt with. As each page is completed, I put a line through it. The benefit of this small discipline is two-fold. First of all, it is efficient. Nothing will be forgotten or overlooked and you can quickly sort out priorities. Secondly and psychologically, the act of writing things down prevents a feeling of muddle. Although your list may never get shorter, since you are constantly adding to it, the line of ticks reassures you that you are keeping on top.

- Endeavour to 'group' your jobs. For instance, if you are calling on your contact in the city, is there another call close by that you might make to save time later?

- Do not allow others to impinge unfairly and wastefully on your time. Chatting about trivialities during working hours will not pay your mortgage.

- Delegate all tasks that do not require your personal attention.

Do try to maintain control. The current theory is that it is dangerous to bottle up tensions, to suppress anger and resentment. But if you want to succeed in business, you will earn no credibility if you throw tantrums all over the place.

As far as possible, face problems and nip them in the bud if you can. If it all gets too much, wait till you get home, beat up a few cushions and make papier-mâché effigies of your tormentors and stick pins in them. Alternatively, write abusive and libellous letters, then burn them.

In addition, accept your femininity. It is not something to be ashamed of or suppressed. If it pleases you, read Catherine

Cookson or *Woman* magazine. Paint your toenails. Three hours spent piping a gateau for your man is not subjugation if that is what you choose to do.

Join a woman's organisation for your industry, profession or small business, and realise that your problems are the same as everyone else's in a similar situation.

Finally, if your pursuits are mostly sedentary, do take up at least one activity which includes some exercise – walking, dancing or keeping fit. It really does work, to relax you, sustain you and prepare you for progressing and winning.

34

THE TAKEOVER BID AND
HOW TO DEFLECT IT

It is interesting to recall that throughout my business life some men have taken great pains to explain to me the reasons for women's inadequacy in matters outside the domestic environment. These reasons are presented as fact, supported by scientific research and experimentation (conducted, no doubt, by men) and always prove something or other deeply significant to the masculine ego.

Conversely, those who are most adamant in their opinion are not necessarily the success stories we all admire. It is quite amazing how many chauvinist pigs have actually managed to bankrupt themselves. Is it not extraordinary therefore that when a woman does get something interesting going, some crazy guy has got to try to take it over!

The ploy begins as follows.

You are invited to lunch. You may agree to lunch because you are unaware of his underlying motives or, like me, just plain greedy, with a particular weakness for little French restaurants that draw the curtains in the middle of the day to produce that unnatural half-light that makes everything so sleepy and relaxed.

Your first mistake!

As you peruse the menu, he says, 'I'll order for you'.

Since you are feeling a little woozy from the fancy aperitif you have just downed at his expense, you allow him to exert his masculinity. Thus he has already compromised you by

[158]

persuading you to eat (i.e. do) what he wants you to eat (i.e. do) He hopes this will be the start of a habit. (Remember your first cigarette?)

He will begin by telling you how he admires you, both as a lovely and sexy woman and also as an acute business mind. He ensures you get enough dressing on your green salad, sends the wine back three times and studies your T-bone minutely for superfluous blood. He will make so much of trivia that the enormity of his proposal when it comes may well escape you.

So be warned.

Ask yourself why.

Why does he need you? What's in it for *you*? Do you want to pay the price of expansion his style? After all, it's ticking along quite nicely as it is. Why rock the boat by taking on a partner?

You try to convey these sentiments to him as tactfully as possible. Your business is very personal to you. You started out with nothing and built it up yourself. You planned and schemed and prospered. How can you, after all these years of going it alone, suddenly have to start accounting for your actions to a partner?

His misinterpretation is deliberate.

'You really have no confidence in yourself, have you, my dear?' While you are recovering from this snide dig, he will press on relentlessly, having thoroughly got into the part.

Now you must take yourself firmly in hand. You have seen his dastardly ploy for what it is and there's no deal. So you retaliate with valid reasons why you don't believe that taking on a partner (or a *passenger*), moving into larger premises and doubling your staff will make you a happier and more fulfilled person, let alone put an extra £10,000 in the bank each year.

He will now get really nasty. He will point out that although you are indeed a lovely and sexy woman, that is *all* you are. You do not possess a business brain (despite his earlier admiration for it). Why, you practically apologise for taking an order!

You need some salesmanship injected into the business.

After all, if you were any good at all, you would be turning over much more than £100,000 per year.

So he wants to pick your brain then kick you down to secretary status, does he?

Tell him he can keep his Bombe Surprise.

You have deflected the Takeover Bid.

35

MAKING IT A BETTER WORLD FOR EVERYONE

Many of the women I have talked to are concerned with the environment and the future prospects of the young, and are busy with sponsorships and charity work. I am not suggesting that generosity is a particularly female trait: on the contrary, there are many wonderfully altruistic businessmen, not least the London taxi drivers who organise the annual day trip for underprivileged children. Yet the most inventive, most original concept of caring must surely be credited to Rennie Fritchie, Management Consultant.

Rennie Fritchie

Rennie's background was not conducive to progress. She left school at 15 after an accident, with no O-levels and no education, yet now she teaches at universities!

Rennie was married at 18 and started a family. Ten years later she was a single parent with a son of eight and another of 6 to support. For a while she did part-time jobs, anything and everything, till an insurance company took her on as a receptionist. The company relocated, and while she was waiting for her smart, new reception area to be constructed, Rennie did lots of other jobs around the company.

This gave her an opportunity to prove herself. She was

promoted to P/A and moved into administration – eventually being entrusted with organisation of the sales force. On the basis of this experience she moved to another insurance company and was selected to train *its* sales force.

'I then got into the Industrial Training Board on administration and became head of the video studio,' says Rennie, 'I began to become more and more involved in training and development, especially women's development, and eventually it developed into a full-time job. So I became a training adviser.'

The next company Rennie worked for, the Social Ecology Association, decided it wanted a British-based consultancy. It set up a partnership of three people, and Rennie stayed with them for about three years, before deciding to set up her own consultancy.

'So I went ahead and after two years I expanded considerably and now I have three associates.'

The Rennie Fritchie Consultancy – not just for profit company

The philosophy of the business is based upon the concept that *every* human being has possible growth and development. To demonstrate, Rennie explained with a story, a *true* one.

'Do you know the story from the *Encyclopaedia Britannica* about Tutankhamen? In the tomb of Tutankhamen they found certain grains of seed and these were taken out and planted. After all those years locked up in the tomb – they *grew*. All they needed were the right balanced conditions.

'When we train people who are at the crossroads, we get them to look at the current situation, to try to understand exactly what has led them to this point. Find out what are the real possibilities, then work in a positive way – so that you begin to develop a vision . . .'

Rennie has a unique three-tier system for charging her clients.

Full-fee-paying clients

These are her 'blue-chip' customers, like Marks & Spencer, an account she won through personal recommendation. She is now responsible for some of the company's training and has just finished a film for the BBC on assertiveness with M & S staff.

'I charge them what is the going rate for a good consultant, to organise management and individuals.'

Half-fee paying customers

Private individuals, voluntary organisations and educational establishments come into this category.

Gift work

Individuals or organisations who have no money don't pay.

'Not that my blue-chip accounts would use me simply for altruistic reasons,' says Rennie. 'They use me because it is good work.'

'A not just for profit company' – not all businesses can justify their slogans, but the Rennie Fritchie Consultancy certainly can . . . and does!

Rennie also runs another small company called Back Up – a support service for small businesses, staffed by part-time women returners.

HINTS FOR THE EXECUTIVE BUSINESSWOMAN

1 Do believe in yourself, even when others denigrate you. Most put-downs serve one purpose: the attempted inflation of the other party's ego.

2 Do assert yourself. This can be done most effectively by making allowances for the other person's point of view, but keeping calm and sticking firmly to your own. It is most disarming to listen carefully, nod your head thoughtfully and concede, 'I quite understand what you're saying, *but* . . .'

3 Do forgive yourself. You have acted in good faith and you are entitled to make mistakes, false judgments and wrong decisions. After all, people who never *try* cannot *fail*.

4 Do accept you are not superwoman. Take one thing at a time. Learn and grow at your own pace. You don't have to be better than a man. Just craftier.

5 Use every method possible to improve your confidence and enhance your style. If you panic inwardly and never know what to do with your hands during confrontations, take a course in public speaking. Your reactions are natural, but control *can* be learned and acquired.

LEADERSHIP STYLES

Women's leadership styles may differ, yet there seem to be certain consistencies – a softer, more realistic approach to their subordinates, the ability to 'make allowances' and a willingness to tackle staff problems at the root rather than deal with them by opting out.

Anne Watts, National Westminster Bank

'At this stage in women's business development, there is still a considerable amount of idealism, i.e. that when women finally reach the top, they will in some way behave differently. They will be more caring, concerned with the human as well as the financial aspects of business, and refrain from dealing in the male politics of hypocrisy and lying.

'There is certainly some evidence already to support the view that women have a different leadership style.'

Anne's style is decidedly one of integrity and straight thinking. She is brisk, businesslike, to the point, yet has the enviable quality of making the truth palatable, even when it is not quite what one wishes to hear!

Patricia Jones, P.J. Employment

'We're a lot more sensitive to other people's feelings than men. A lot of women in managerial positions have come through the ranks. I know this can be true for men, but in general, for every two leaps a man makes, a woman must make six or seven. Let's face it, many start off as secretaries, so they are more aware of the problems.

'One thing I always try to do is to be honest about my mistakes. I might try to gloss over my minor errors, but I'll always admit if I've made a serious blunder. I think that is important, and I think my staff respect me for it.'

Maureen Sampson, Knightsbridge Antiques

'Sometimes I feel that I intimidate my staff, although I do not intend to. What I do try to do is to give praise when it is earned and I have found that certain employees do respond well to this.

'I also believe in supporting them if they show promise, and I recently sent one of my carpenter/joiners to college. I am pleased to say that he was the "second to top" student.'

Deryn Stewart, Wedgwood Hotel Ware

'One of the reasons I can get people to work well for me is because they know I would never ask them to do something I wouldn't do myself, which I think is very different from a man's attitude.

'I know it's important to delegate, but when it gets tough I am always prepared to come down and "muck in". This gives other people, especially young people, much more incentive to motivate themselves.'

[166]

Deryn is only 27, slim, dark and very pretty. But beneath the fragile looks, there is a sense of determination and stoicism far beyond her years.

Sally Buckley, Philips Industries

Sally is a senior buyer and as such must be able to work well under tremendous pressure. Her clear-thinking style comes through in her precise analysis of her own leadership style.

'You must earn respect as a leader, motivate people to work as a team and with a common aim in view. I think this is very important. It is all part of a whole, these three things – respect, motivation and aim. I see them as circles that overlap.'

Marilyn Hunter, Hunters Chartered Accountants

The nature of her business dictates that Marilyn must aim to employ only people of the highest calibre.

'I am careful about whom I take on, because I mostly subcontract and cannot be watching over them all the time. I have to rely on my assistants to an enormous degree. Professional indemnity insurance is expensive; it has to be by law. If a mistake was made and I was sued, it could cost thousands.

'I do try to motivate people by adding interest to the work; for instance, I like to give them background information about the clients. If they have a problem, I prefer them to approach me directly and supply me with copious notes, some of which may be disregarded, than a minimum of information which could result in my missing something important.

'I never hesitate to pass work back if it's not good enough. In return for high standards of work, I am prepared to pay well and offer reasonably flexible hours.'

Maggie of Warlingham

'In a small business, where we are working closely together, it's got to be on a friendship basis to get the best out of each other. One employee has been with me for seven years – we're friends. Tolerance levels. have got to be there. I don't delegate – we are all in it together for the same outcome. They need a job and they like to work with me.'

Rennie Fritchie, Management Consultant

'I believe in leading both from in front and beside. Leadership from in front demonstrates its own role model, by example, in a style that is charismatic, inspirational, larger than life, so that people are involved and follow.

'To lead beside means to actually sit with the person you are working with and be a human being – and *do it wholeheartedly.*'

Rennie believes in applying her considerable experience in remedial training to her own situation.

'It's not a good thing to pigeon-hole people. It is better to help people work out what is best for them and achieve what is reasonable. Help them to set their own goals.

'Of course, there are personal disappointments, when you are let down, but then you have to pick yourself up and start all over again.'

GETTING OUR ACT TOGETHER

I have enjoyed writing this book and meeting all the marvellous women who have contributed to it. For every piece of knowledge or experience I have sunk into these pages I have learned something new.

I have met women with totally different life-styles, different approaches, different ideas. Yet in every case there are consistencies, a spirited refusal to be put down even in the face of tremendous odds. It isn't ever easy being in a minority. Everywhere I have looked I have found staunchness, determination and courage – and in spite of all that there is still room for compassion.

As time goes on matters will improve. They have already. As one young female representative said to me recently, 'My sales director is a woman. If I got into any difficulties regarding sexism or serious harassment, I know I would have the back-up. She's been there and she wouldn't let me down.'

Emmeline Pankhurst would have been proud.

Let us end with the words of Rennie Fritchie: 'Find out what are the real possibilities, then work in a positive way – so that you begin to develop a vision . . .'

CROSSWORD

Test your knowledge with this crossword. Answers will be found on p. 175.

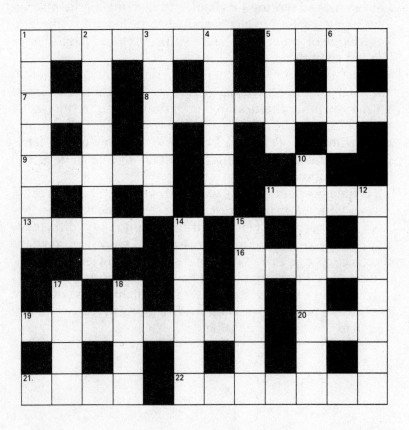

Crossword

ACROSS

1 People who are poseurs do this (7).

5 You will severely cramp your style if you always play it this way (4).

7 What you are aiming to be (3).

8 Your suppliers must provide these (8).

9 Precedes the certification of your accounts (5).

11 The exercise of power to prevent (4).

13 To locate or place in a specific area (4).

16 Inappropriate (5).

19 It is not sufficient just to get your new venture off the ground. You must also do this (8).

20 The very core of your existence, your progression and your determination to win (3).

21 During bad times a lot will depend upon your ability to do this with regard to your aims and intentions (4).

22 Way of dealing with a long and complicated report (7).

DOWN

1 Expenditures (7).

2 Speed up (8).

3 Let us hope that the sum total of these exceed that of your liabilities (6).

4 An especially helpful characteristic for a pauper starting up in business (6).

5 A bargain (4).

6 It is said that a business lunch can never be this (4).

10 To do this you must first plan your strategy (3–5).

12 The consequences of your actions (7).

14 A list of errors (6).

15 The main purpose of this book is to help you become one (6).

17 Central trading place (4).

18 If you want to succeed, you must contend with this (4).

INDEX

Solution to crossword on p. 170.